A Woman's Journey Home
14 Keys to Ascending to the Next Dimension

Tonika M. Breeden

CANNONPUBLISHING

A Woman's Journey Home

14 Keys to Ascending to the Next Dimension

Tonika M. Breeden

CANNONPUBLISHING

DEDICATION

This book is dedicated to the Boss Chick who is focused on her hustle instead of healing her soul.

The Ministry Leader who is dedicated, disciplined, consistent and obedient…yet also very tired.

The Single Mother struggling to get past her past and raise her children without becoming bitter.

The Career Woman, climbing the corporate ladder but feeling like an imposter.

The Wounded Woman still caught up in the denial, delusion and distraction of counterfeit love.

The Powerful Woman who has excelled in purpose but has few sisters she can call "friend."

To every woman who felt that she was either "not enough" or "too much".

To every woman that has felt unseen, unsought for and uncertain.

This book is for you….

This book is for me.

CONTENTS

Introduction.. III

Part One: The Journey Home

Chapter 1: *Stick a Fork In Me! I am Done* 1
Chapter 2: *Home is Where the Heart is* 5
Chapter 3: *Get Real and Be Healed* from Unregulated Emotions.............. 13
Chapter 4: *The Fever, Fret & Frenzy of the Flesh* 19
Chapter 5: *We Go Low* 25
Chapter 6: *Get Out of Dead-End Relationships* 29
Chapter 7: *Does it Really Matter?* 35

Part Two: The Next Dimension

Chapter 8: *Activating the Spirit of Completion* 41
Chapter 9: *We Walk by Faith & Vision, Not Feelings & Sight* 47
Chapter 10: *The Small Decisions Turn* the Wheels of Destiny.................53
Chapter 11: Praise & Worship: The Frequency of Heaven..................... 57
Chapter 12: Surrender to the Season. What You Resist Persists.................. 61
Chapter 13: We Move from Glory to Glory 65
Chapter 14: The Five Deadly "I's" That Prevent True Connection.............. 71

Conclusion: You are Worthy! 83
Endnotes 85
Acknowledgements 87
About the Author..89

INTRODUCTION

After this I looked, and, behold, a door was opened in heaven: and the first voice which I heard was as it were of a trumpet talking with me; which said, Come up hither, and I will shew thee things which must be hereafter.

-Revelations 4:1

The word of the Lord came to John, the Baptist saying - Come up higher! There was an open door set before him. It was there, waiting. However, John had to come up higher to walk through that door. He couldn't remain stationary or sit in the same position without any movement and expect for the door to open.

He couldn't see what God wanted to show him by remaining at the lower level. He would not have the proper context or understanding of what God wanted to reveal to him from the current point of view that he had.

Note that God didn't stoop down to where he was, John had to come up hither. God had a future vision – a future reality to show John that would impact the earth. Yet for John to properly receive and perceive this vision, he had to remove himself from a lower existence, a lower level of understanding, a lower level of perception to be in position to receive the insight, understanding and revelation at the higher level.

The pull or draw that you feel deep in your soul to be different, to stand out, to expand, to rise and be a better woman is the calling of God on your life. The calling propels, pulls and pushes you to "come up higher." It is the deep inward call of your spirit that tugs at you, prompts you, and nudges at you in those quiet moments, gently reminding you that it's not over. There is more in you that must come out.

That is what this book is all about. It's about doing whatever it takes in order to come up higher. Coming up higher is indeed a process and a journey. It is not for the faint of heart.

We pray for the elevation of a new level, but oftentimes we underestimate the depth of the struggle and the pain involved in relinquishing the old way of thinking, feeling, being and doing required at that new and higher level that we deeply crave.

i

We look at others whom we perceive to be further along in their journey or who appear to be operating on a higher level than we are and subject ourselves to the pain of comparison and competition.

Without a full understanding of the price and suffering that others have paid to master themselves and maintain at certain levels, we may wrongfully desire what they have or be inwardly insecure because we have not taken the time to surrender and commit to the process.

For many, the entire dynamic of comparison and competition inhibits true growth because it keeps the focus away from personal purpose development and internal healing, but instead the focus is on what other people are doing --- watching, copying them; breeding more insecurity.

On the other hand, many of us gladly embrace the process of coming up higher, but fail to realize that we must first get grounded and back to the basics in terms of our identity and internal healing work that must be done first. The end result of not being grounded in who you are before rising to a new level is a quick descent back into mediocrity, hiding and self-sabotage as soon as the pressure of a new level comes.

To that end, I've divided this book into two sections –Part 1. The Journey Home and Part 2. The Next Dimension. Part 1 is based on the premise that before we can go higher, we must come back home. There is a journey home – home to God and being at home with ourselves in order to be grounded and stabilized enough to survive at the higher levels and altitudes.

In Part two, once we have come back home and are grounded within ourselves and who we are, we are then in position to come up higher into new levels and dimensions with staying power and longevity.

Coming home first enables us to come up higher from a place of confidence and consistency so that we are not "one hit wonders" or "here today and gone today" types of people that never make to any level of influence and impact for the Kingdom of God.

Part 1 deals with foundational principles of dealing with oneself to arrive safely at a new level and Part 2 provides key principles that must be adhered to in order to maintain and sustain that new higher level.

Without having an accurate understanding of the journey home and the call to come up higher, the temptation and the struggle would be to stay in a perpetual state of limbo – neither fully at home or at the next level, but simply in a state of distraction and discouragement.

It's time for you to come home. It's time for you to ascend to the next dimension.

Heed the call.

Part 1

THE JOURNEY HOME

Chapter 1

STICK A FORK IN ME! I AM DONE

"Before you act, listen.
Before you read, think.
Before you spend, earn.
Before you criticize, wait.
Before you pray, forgive.
Before you quit, try."
- Ernest Hemmingway

Before you come up higher in your life, your purpose, your finances, your relationships, your calling, and purpose– before you do *anything at all of Kingdom significance, y*ou must come home to God and home to yourself.

Before you can elevate and transform in any area of your life you must come back home to yourself and back home to your place and position as a Child of the Most High God.

If there is any disconnect between you and God or a disconnection within your soul (mind, will and emotions), there is no way you can come up higher without the spirit of self-sabotage taking over.

For as soon as you begin to take the steps to move forward, your emotions will run wild, your mind will scream in fear, and your will becomes superseded by the agenda of the enemy thru distractions.

Disconnection comes under the guise of busyness, delays, emotional numbness, woundedness and unprocessed pain. Disconnection comes hidden in the vague underlying sense of anxiety and restlessness.

Disconnection secretly hides out behind being a lone ranger or it is more blatant in the spirit of comparison and competition we often see in ministry and business circles.

Wherever there is any degree of emotional, spiritual, and mental disconnection you can rest assured that somewhere along the journey, you have lost your way and need to come home. Home to yourself and Home to God. Let me share a bit of my Come Home Journey.

Stick a Fork in Me – I am Done!

It was the constant tension of having to perpetually keep myself in check emotionally so that I didn't speak out of order or ill-advisedly and create more chaos, pain and unanticipated side effects.

It was the pressure of having to hear and see things that I could not verbalize or express but had to hold to myself and pray. This was difficult.

It was the realization that people who smiled at me really didn't like me that much. It is hard for me to fake so I grin, bear and be nice anyway but keep my distance. It was the sudden realization that somehow while walking in purpose my circle of friends grew smaller. This was painful.

It was the power of the prophetic words over my life that were beginning to manifest. With joy and amazement, I watched them unfold. But I soon realized that for every prophetic Word, there is a test attached. For every Word spoken, there will be a battle.

It was the literal running in the streets, (from pillar to post like the old folks used to say) – picking up my sons from their various practices, going to the grocery store, picking up fast food or running home to jump on a conference call or prepare for an upcoming speech.

Oh by the way, I also had to check my phone *yet again* for another work email that came through that I must attend to. Sometimes it was just overwhelming.

It was the brief moments when I would do a live video on social media when I received what I knew was a word or download from God that I should share, so I would have to find time to prepare and deliver it. I fell off the wagon and wasn't always obedient. Truth be told, this occurred often.

It was the niggling sense that some people were acting strange, weird or bizarre towards me and I didn't understand why. It hurt. It also hurt that I probably acted weird and strange to them too.

It was because I was hurting and overwhelmed and just didn't want to talk or be bothered sometimes. Then I would feel *guilty*. I wanted genuine connections and friendships, but I knew I didn't have the capacity to maintain a bunch of connections at that time. I didn't have the emotional capacity for multiple friendships and different people pulling on me. I would always pray (and still do) Lord, send me the right people for me in this season that can add value to me and I to them. Help me discern the fake, weird or insecure ones and not be leery or intimidated myself with my own insecurities by the right ones. God help me.

It was feeling guilty when I could see my sons and I going into our separate rooms, me to work on my laptop, them to watch TV and get on PlayStation. Here we are – together, but not *together*.

It was the realization that I had a twelfth-grade son on my hands who still was not where he needed to be academically and now as we sit on the cusp of graduation and I am wondering how I am going to get this boy out of my house and to college. I had a hard time trying to get my mind around the money involved because scholarships are not handed out to "C" or "D" students. It was stressful!

It was having to release a potential #Bae that I knew would be a serious distraction and possibly cause me to compromise. Even when I knew it was the right thing to do, it still was not easy. Especially, when I liked him.

It was fighting off the overthought, reading into things that weren't there, judgments and criticisms against others that the enemy would try to plant in my mind during my lowest moments.

It was the eye-opening experience of realizing that all men in ministry truly do not walk in integrity. It was eye-opening when a man of God approached me and said certain things making me feel that somehow, he must have thought that I would go along with his ungodly ways. The unmitigated gall!

It was the newness of a new level. New connections. Stepping Out. Mistakes made. Lessons learned.

Last, but not least, I realize that now my jeans are fitting more snuggly than usual, I have more aches and pains and I receive my credit card statement and see that I have accumulated more debt than I realized.

I still had not generated the revenue I thought I would by this time last year.

It was *everything*.

So yes, finally I was done. Stick a fork in me, I WAS DONE! The last few weeks leading up to year-end had finally wound down. I was *so ready* to stop the madness. From speaking engagements, keeping up with social media and appearances (we all know that we present a pseudo fake version of reality on social media), working a very demanding full-time job in which it was all I could do to keep myself from going off on people.

It was then that I finally decided, "Girl, it's time for you to come home."

Chapter 2

HOME IS WHERE THE HEART IS

Guard your heart above all else, for it determines the course of your life.
– Proverbs 4:23 (NLT)

*Y*our heart is your center point. Your heart must be guarded and kept safe. It must be monitored and carefully watched. It must be placed in the hands of the one who created it – God.

As the old saying goes, charity begins at home. Since your home is where the heart it, let's look at the definition of Home:

Home (def): The Place where one lives permanently especially as a member of a family or household; to go to the intended or correct position; the place where someone or something flourishes, where it originates and is typically found; the finishing point, the clear, significant, "on point" understanding (ex, she brought it "home")

Clearly, we are not talking about a physical location, but a rather position in the spirit. I'm talking about a spiritual posture of the heart of coming back home to God as well as yourself. This usually requires facing some painful truths. It usually requires making a turn. You can't stay where you are and expect to elevate to a higher position, without first becoming grounded, back to base and in position if you have been out of alignment and out of order for a long time.

Similar to your physical house or home, your emotional home needs daily cleaning and maintenance for comfort, safety and rest. How do you feel when your home is out of order and messy? What happens when you are away from home too long or if you go too long without putting things away and things start to pile up?

I know for me personally, if I let things get too far gone because I am too busy and preoccupied with other activities, my home will get messy. If I allow myself to become overly fatigued that things will not get clean and I suffer the consequences. I am not able to fully rest and enjoy my home when it's out of order. I feel unsettled, scattered and distracted when the energy of my home is not right, and I have gone too long without getting things in proper order.

As it is in the natural, so it is in the spirit. When you fail to heal and order on the inside – in your soul daily, emotional baggage such as unprocessed pain, daily offenses, negativity, and fear will pile up. If we go too long in this state, without taking the time with God to unpack and heal with Him we can become spiritually and emotionally unclean.

We will attempt to serve our families and minister to other people from this unkept and scattered emotional place. It causes us to not be fully present in the moment by attempting to numb our pain and issues with more busyness and distractions. We wind up fretful, joyless, lacking peace, full of overwhelm, impatience and anxiety.

This is what happens when the home of the heart – our emotional and spiritual base becomes unclean and out of alignment.

Before I get into the principles of coming up higher ------- let's be clear – you must come home to God and come home to yourself FIRST.

CHOKING DOWN THE TRUTH

The truth hurts, but it doesn't kill. Lies may please but they don't heal.
- Unknown

There is also another quote I heard somewhere that states we generally find a lie very palatable and easy to swallow. However, we find the truth to be very bitter and hard to choke down. Thus, we avoid the truth altogether or if we chose to receive the truth about ourselves, we only have the capacity to sip it little by little.

Yet, we read clearly in the scripture about how the God we serve is a God of truth. There is no lie in Him. As a matter of fact, those of us who claim to follow Christ have literally surrendered our lives to the Way of Truth. We read in John 14:6 that He is The Way, The Truth and the Life. We also read earlier in the book of John that we will know the Truth and the Truth will set us free (John 8:32).

6

Truth be told (pun intended), there is no way we can claim to be Christians and claim to walk authentically with God but somehow manage to avoid choking down the hard, bitter truth about ourselves.

There is no way we can follow Christ, yet readily and swiftly receive and believe the lies of the enemy, who according to Christ in John 8:44 is the Father of Lies.

Take a moment to read and reflect on this one verse - Psalm 51: 6

Behold, you desire truth in the inner being; make me therefore to know wisdom in my inmost heart.

Five key words – Truth, inner being, inmost and heart.

Truth must be deeply implanted in our hearts and received before we can know wisdom. Truth must be revealed within our inner man so that we can make the necessary adjustments to change our lives in accordance with the truth. Once I hear a truth, I am now responsible for the application of that truth to my life.

Truth once heard, swallowed and received into the heart has a profound, life altering effect. Once you have received Truth, you can never go back to being the same. Take a moment and get a visual of a totally stretched out rubber band in your mind. Once that rubber band has been stretched beyond its original capacity, it can never shrink back to being the same. The truth has a similar impact upon souls once it is deeply received.

Facing and receiving the truth about where we are, how we got there, what we are doing in our lives, what we have done, the status of our relationships, our body temples and our purpose is the very first and most important step to coming home. Coming Home is the process of coming back to the truth.

It is the process of letting go of the lies we have swallowed in our struggles to cope with life, to go along to get along, to not feel pain and to make things happen in our own strength.

FACING THE GOOD TRUTH

An unexamined life is not worth living. – Plato

In this moment, I encourage you to pause and reflect over your life. Think of and write down at least ten things you are proud of – when you shed forty pounds., went back to school and got your degree, married the love of your life, had beautiful children, started that business or ministry, wrote the book, survived job loss, unemployment, sickness, abandonment, betrayal yet you are still in your right mind and so forth.

This too, is an important part in facing and acknowledging truth. It is also an acknowledgement that yes, God has a purpose for my life. Yes, my life matters! Yes, I am worthy! Yes, if I did it before, I can do it again with God on my side!

Facing the truth about your accomplishments does several things. 99% of us under celebrate. We do not properly thank God or acknowledge ourselves for the hard-won victories we have gained over the years. We work and sweat. We toil and struggle. We fast and pray. Then the big thing happens. We did it and it is done.

We are happy for a moment or two. We post a few pictures on social media and bask in the "likes and hearts". Then just like the life span of a typical social media post (they are only "hot" for a few hours) we scroll right on past the win without adequate acknowledgement.

We fail to allow our souls to actually sit in and soak in the moment. Our souls never get a chance to catch up with all that has been completed and we never learn to nurture and savor the joy that completion brings. This is important.

Why? Because awareness, acknowledgement and documentation (actually writing it down) seals and memorializes your wins in your soul. This comes in handy when you are on the battlefield of ascending to your next level and the enemy of your soul wants to fill your mind with all of your shortcomings, failures, mistakes and areas where you fall short. Intentional acknowledgement comes in handy and gives you ammunition along with the Word of God to fight the battlefield of your mind against you.

Don't do a "drive by social media snapshot" with your victories! Make your list. Write it down. Be thankful. Sit and savor in your victories.

FACING THE UGLY TRUTH

Now that we have adequately faced and acknowledged the good truth – the truth of all of what God has done in our lives, the second step is to face the not-so-good moments. Even within this, there is goodness because on the surface things may *appear* to be bad or a failure, but may actually have been part of God's planning, positioning and training to prepare you to come up higher.

Looking back within the past twelve months of your life, go through each month to see where your energy went. This may require going through your mobile phone, your calendar, your pictures, your social media posts, your journal, etc. but take a few moments and look at your life.

This can be scary. Most people don't like this because again, it can be painful and take you perhaps some places you don't want to go.

Yet, God desires truth in the inward parts. Glossing over, stuffing, hiding, numbing does not make certain events go away. They just sit quietly and simmer in your subconscious and in your heart then right at the most inopportune moment, you are unpleasantly triggered by a current situation because it looked like the past situation and wonder why you had such a strong emotion.

It is because you still have something undealt with that you are stuffing away. In this review we will gently unpack your life so that you can be honest with yourself and God over the last few months. Don't be afraid! It's just a process.

For each month as best as you can remember:

1) Where did the bulk of your time, your emotional, mental, spiritual and financial energy go?
2) Did the people, places and things that you invested your life into increase or decrease you?
3) In looking at your activities and relationships, was it in alignment with what you believe is God's purpose for you?
4) Did the activities and people you spent time with bring you closer to home (with yourself and God's plans) or did it drive you further away?

This is what it means to come home and this is what it looks like when you are really serious about healing and ordering your life so that you can come up higher. God desires truth. Coming home to Him and coming home

9

to ourselves requires honesty. We can't come home or go up higher living a lie!

Let me share a little of what I realized when I went through my calendar and activities over a twelve-month span. I realized that I had a very productive year of growth in my speaking, i.e. - I reached a lot more people, gained visibility on a larger scale, grew in ways and stretched myself more than I thought. But on the flip side the busier I became, the less time I had to deal with emotional clutter from the various movement I was making. My spiritual home was getting out of order....

Like I mentioned earlier, our inner world – our home is just like a house - if you don't clean emotional clutter it will pile up on you! I found more emotional clutter that needed to be dealt with because I didn't take the time to repent, cleanse and heal as I go.

Overall, I saw that the bulk of my activities were actually in alignment and my energy generally was going in the right direction, but because I still lacked emotional regulation under times of stress and pressure, I became easily offended, misinterpreted situations, held on to hurts and it was all related to the stress of actually coming up higher and being elevated in the calling of God.

I learned that when you elevate, your soul must be able to handle the pressure of it without weakening emotionally, being a wreck, losing it, feeling some kind of way, and getting overwhelmed.

I learned that when we ask God for bigger and better, we must have the emotional resiliency and fortitude to handle the pressure, stress and warfare that comes along with it. There is a higher degree of discipline and focus required the deeper and higher you move in your purpose. Can you handle the mantle?

I realized that I couldn't go around telling people to Get Real and Be Healed if I was not getting real and being healed continuously myself as things occurred. Remember, life is life. Things happen. Getting real and being healed is a continuous process. You can actually be healed in an area and then something happens and there is another layer of healing that needs to happen. You can be delivered in one area, and God shows you another area.

You can think you are healed in something and then get in a relationship --- not necessarily romantic and realize the thing you thought you were

10

healed from is now being tested in the new relationship and you find yourself still triggered! This is the reality – LIFE IS MESSY. HEALING IS MESSY. We need to always find our way home to God and Truth.

To do this requires the "R" Word—people don't like this word REPENTANCE:

In his book, Queenlogy, Bishop R. C. Blacks, Jr. states that repentance is defined as "a change of mind from evil to good or from good to better. Repentance is the simple act of changing your mind and correcting your course to match your new thinking." From Complete Word Study Bible – Queenology /Bishop R.C. Blakes p. 25.

Craig Groeschel in his book *Divine Direction* states that "The word repentance literally means to change course; to stop walking in one direction and return to God and his path for us."

For us, repentance simply means to come back to being the woman of God you are called to be. It means to come back home and come up higher.

This means making your appointment with God and praying – cry out to Him for the help, healing and deliverance you need. This looks like openly and verbally talking to God out loud --- *not* silent prayers. We are talking about verbalized and spoken prayer. We are talking about writing it out if necessary.

There is something about hearing your own voice and your own words coming out of your mouth when you acknowledge where you are and your desire to come home that is very powerful.

There is something about writing things down that seals and crystalizes the thoughts which in turn brings substance and clarity. It's called working out your own soul salvation. It's when you release everything that holds you back and from coming up higher. Like Paul in Philippians 3:13-14, we know that we don't have it all together yet, but we repent and forget those things which are behind us and keep pressing forward to what lies ahead. Yes, it is a press, but well worth it.

Now that we have laid the foundation of facing the truth and making the decision to repent and turn, we will now look at concrete and practical ways to actually walk this out. Over the course of the next few weeks, we will dig deeply into twelve key ways in which we first come home to God and ourselves and secondly come up higher in how we show up in our lives. The

11

first seven keys deal with coming home and the last seven deal with coming up higher.

1. Do you see glimpses of yourself in my story of being "Done!"?
2. What good truths about yourself and not so good did you realize when you looked at where your energy has been flowing the past few months?
3. Are you truly ready to unpack, heal and come home?

"Heavenly Father, I take this time to honor myself and honor you by taking a holy pause to examine my life and come back home to you and to myself. I choose today to courageously face the truth about myself without shame, guilt or condemnation. I receive your forgiveness and love. I choose to receive your grace to fill in every gap in my life. I choose to come home. In Jesus' Name. Amen."

Chapter 3

GET REAL AND BE HEALED
FROM UNREGULATED EMOTIONS

"When a woman has no emotional control, she is socially and relationally vulnerable. She is compromised by her own emotions...If you don't have control of your emotions, someone else does. When you're out of control, some else is in control. When you protect your emotions, you own your personal power and can dictate the atmosphere around you..."

– Bishop R. C. Blakes

*U*nregulated emotions and wounds keep us vulnerable and exposed. We can't come up higher unless we are grounded and centered emotionally. To be grounded and centered means that we are actively dealing with and facing any emotional pain from the past and current pain that may appear in our normal, everyday life.

A lot of times some of the negative emotions and wounds that we carry are not always a result of some deep, dark pain or secret issue that occurred in our past.

It's the little things. We read in Song of Solomon 2:15 that it is the little foxes that spoil the vine. The daily aggravations and annoyances. The small and petty inconveniences. A word spoken. A post on social media. The way someone looked at you. Feeling slighted or overlooked. The tone of his or her voice when they said this or that. The list goes on.

It's the little things that pile up and get us in trouble. The irony is that the busier you become the more likely you are to carry around a bag in your heart of a bunch of little things that somehow pile up into a big heart issue. If you are not careful to confess (1 John 1:9) and ask God to clean your heart (Ps. 51:10), you will eventually wind up carrying a huge load of emotional pain and offense in your heart and wonder how it got there.

At this point, let me make a PSA – a Public Service Announcement:
You are a human being.

Yes, you read right! A human. As a human being living on this earth, you will have emotional and spiritual pain. Anyone in pain deserves to be treated humanely.

Humane treatment is defined as "having or showing compassion or benevolence". Therefore, the humane thing to do as a human being with pain is to treat yourself like a human – with kindness and compassion.

It means to actually give yourself the dignity and respect to honor the fact that as a human and a child of God that you have pain and that you deserve to feel, heal and process your pain in a healthy way.

However, what we do is the opposite. We do not treat ourselves humanely when we are in pain.

What we tend to do is to numb the pain on busyness, activities, drugs, shopping, sex, overwork until we eventually break down and pay the price for it in our bodies or have an actual emotional meltdown.

I love this quote that I heard from Shannon Tanner:

"Expression is life. Repression is death. Every time we repress our truth we die a little on the inside. What you will not speak out, your body will act out. Your body will break down and pay the price."

Your body acts out in the extra weight, the aches, the pains, the medications and so on.

Repression looks like numbing, hiding, perpetrating, pretending, and over-spiritualizing our situation instead of simply getting real by admitting that we are hurt and need healing. What you will not express and own as your truth, your body will break down and pay the price. Pain is a teacher and indicator, we don't sit in it, but we feel it and walk through it.

When we avoid and repress our pain we are treating ourselves inhumanely. We are treating ourselves as less than a human and less than a child of God sometimes without realizing it.

Remember this: Pain is a teacher. It comes to *pass*; not to *stay*. Unregulated, runaway emotions in a woman is always a sign of unprocessed pain or emotional wounds that needs to be dealt with. In Proverbs 18:14, we clearly read that a wounded spirit is hard to bear. It is not always comfortable to be in a close relationship with someone who is wounded. If you are reading this and deeply desire to be married in the future, yet you

14

have a wounded spirit, it is a repellent to attracting and sustaining healthy love.

Processing and healing is *not a* quick fix. We want to rush through healing and doing our soul work simply because we don't want to feel it. A lot of times we want God to heal us quickly and give us a man or answer our prayer in a certain way. We want God to make us financially rich with little effort or work – just like a get rich quick scheme. Your outward life is an expression of your inner world. It all ends and begins with you and everything flows from you.

When we hang onto pain and refuse to deal with it, it's like hoarding the hurt. Often we are bitter but we go around telling everyone and attempting to convince ourselves that we are okay by saying things in conversations like, "I'm fine", "I'm not mad", "I've forgiven him/her/them" …but yes you still are!

When we hoard the hurt, again we are not treating ourselves with compassion and dignity - - *humanely*, but as less than a human under the guise of being in control and moving on quickly all because we don't want to unpack and feel that pain. We just want to keep right on moving.

Anything swept under the rug is still in the house. In other words, if you sweep a big piece of trash under a rug instead of removing it, it's still sitting in your home. It didn't go anywhere. We can't keep sweeping unresolved pain under the rugs of our spiritual and emotional houses and pretend they don't exist. The emotional piles of pain and hurt still sit there growing and festering into something much bigger than your original problem the longer they are left unattended.

We can't cure what we keep covered. Large gaping emotional wounds can't be covered with an overly spiritualized, tiny Band-Aid. They need to be exposed to the air of the Holy Spirit and within the context of confidential, safe and godly relationships in order to heal.

Having a safe space to confess faults, i.e., the sins, struggles, unhealed parts of ourselves that are not pretty one to another so that we can be healed is an instruction and strategy as found in James 5:16 "Confess you sins to each other and pray for each other so that you may be healed. The earnest prayer of a righteous person has great power and produces wonderful results." In other words, we must actually open our mouths and say something about what is going on with us to a safe person (note the key word is "safe". Not everyone is qualified, have the maturity, and discretion to hear your story) in order to heal and order our lives. As the old folks used to say, "closed mouths do not get fed…"

As women, we must face feelings with courage and honesty instead of repressing or avoiding them or minimizing them by acting super spiritual. When we face them honestly we become *stronger and heal faster*. This requires compassion and ability to be kind to ourselves and feel the emotions (like a normal human) and let them pass through without getting stuck.

Allowing yourself to feel difficult emotions so that you can heal in a healthy way is very crucial. It is not compassionate to yourself to hold back the tears when you need to cry, to be tough when you are genuinely soft, to forever keep your guard up (even when it's safe to take it down), and to always be in control so that you are incapable of being vulnerable.

Living this way over time makes you hard-hearted. However, allowing yourself to actually feel your feelings without getting stuck in them and without making life-altering decisions while still in them is compassionate and wise. It is inhumane and not of God to pretend.

Yes, we are instructed to be strong in the Lord and in the power of His might and utilize our spiritual armor but this is within the context of a spiritual battle not within the context of healing and dealing with your emotions. After the battle is won, you still have to face yourself and process the battle and that's where the healing is!

Let's face it. The majority of your emotional wounds were created within the context of relationships --- family relationships, friendships and romantic relationships. You must be willing to do the inner work to be richer, fuller and freer on the inside so that you will create room in your heart for the authentic Kingdom connections to arrive in your life, whether it is a romantic purpose partner for marriage or other relationships critical to your growth and development as a woman.

Remember, some of the relationship dynamics and emotional coping mechanisms that have served you up to this point in your life, are no longer working for you right now, or else you would not keep repeating the same struggles and patterns.

Whatever kinds of behaviors, thinking patterns, belief systems, language and words that served you in your pit seasons, i.e., the seasons of life when you were immature and out of order, struggling to survive, living in and believing in lies, does not belong in the Palace of our Purpose.

In her book, The Prosperous Soul, Dr. Cindy Trimm states that "Spiritual [and] emotional.... growth require that we exchange our childhood scripts for adult strategies." In other words, we must learn adult emotional coping strategies and give up the childish defense mechanisms we picked up along the way if we expect to fully become the women of God we are called to be.

For me to operate in the new levels and realms God is calling me to, I must let go of my immature emotional coping strategies. I must replace these scripts with the adult strategies of a full-grown, mature Woman of God who can be trusted to navigate and process her emotions in a healthy way even under pressure and while in pain.

We must give up repressing. numbing, lashing out and other inhumane and immature behaviors in order for God to trust us at higher realms of influence, affluence and leadership without it crushing us.

In Proverbs 25:28 we read, He (or she) who has no rule over his own spirit is like a city that is broken down and without walls (AMPC). Ruling your spirit calls for emotional regulation and the ability to walk by the spirit instead of feelings.

If we are emotionally unstable, when the increased pressure and altitude of new elevations, increase and levels come, we will fall apart. We could self-sabotage because we "feel some kind of way" about someone that God intends to use to bless us. We could become so overwhelmed emotionally that we don't know how to calm down, unpack and heal with God privately thus we end up falling apart publicly and hindering our witness as ambassadors of Christ.

REFLECTIVE QUESTIONS

1. Ask God to reveal the areas where you are still unhealed and broken.
2. Make a commitment to no longer run, resist and repress feeling the pain by hustling, being overly busy, overeating and other hiding and defense mechanisms that you are doing.
3. Give God access to all parts of your heart and soul
4. Ask God to make you whole and complete, lacking in nothing.

"Heavenly Father, you already know the areas of my heart and soul that are unhealed. I ask by the power of your Holy Spirit to come in and work within me, what I cannot do for myself. I surrender to your guidance in my healing process. I give you access to all parts of my heart and soul. I declare and decree that I am whole and complete, pure and secure, lacking in nothing. Amen."

Chapter 4

THE FEVER, FRET & FRENZY OF THE FLESH

"We take care of ourselves; we make our own plans and struggle to make things happen our way, in our timing. This describes the natural way, the "normal" way most people live. It is a way that produces every kind of misery. We struggle, get frustrated, fail and end up weary and worn-out most of the time. We are confused and defeated and have no peace and joy."

- Joyce Meyer

*A*s the saying goes, "Been there, done that and got the t-shirts..."
Oh yes indeed. I am *very* familiar with the lifestyle Joyce Meyer describes above. I will have a plan in my head (or written out) of how my day is supposed to go, what I planned to accomplish, and all that I wanted to happen. Even though I prayed about it and asked God to help me, once my personal zeal and deep desire for things to happen take over, unbeknownst to me, God has already quietly stepped out.

I wouldn't realize it until I realize I am frustrated, raising my voice at the boys again (pray my strength), still forcing and trying to make something happen when I am bone tired, with no energy, pushing against my own body.

I wouldn't realize it until I find myself very impatient and having a bad case of road rage on the way home from work.

It wasn't until I said a cuss word under my breath in the church parking lot when I couldn't find my keys as the cold wind was hitting me through my clothes.

I wouldn't realize that I was operating from the fret and frenzy of my flesh until I found myself in overthought, confusion, competition and in other people's lanes.

I would open up my Bible and land on 1 Corinthians 13 where Paul describes what real love is or Galatians 5:22 where he describes the nine fruit of the spirit – Love, joy, peace, patience, kindness, goodness, faithfulness, gentleness and self-control.

Suddenly, I am acutely aware by the power of the Holy Spirit (it was Him who caused me to "somehow" land on these scriptures in my Bible.)I did not flow in these fruits very well and that my love walk was quite shaky and undeveloped.

But I have all of these goals, visions, plans and dreams --- you know, the hustle and the grind. Everybody is an author, entrepreneur, and a speaker these days. Everybody has a webinar, a course, a masterclass, a private Facebook group. Everybody has an event or a conference. Everybody has some sort of "hustle" and/or "grind" that they are working on.

Everybody.

So, I too, must jump on the bandwagon and burn myself out in the fret, fever and frenzy of my flesh trying to make something happen in my own strength that only God can do in his timing through His power and strength.

Over time, I have come to realize that every action must have intention. Every action I take must be taken from the space and the pace of God's grace and not my personal zeal and fleshly energy. Every time I operate in my own energy, there is an entirely different set of results than when I operate in God's grace and timing.

What I have come to understand is that when I am not all gung-ho trying to get something done, but rather I am slowing myself down to receive instruction from Him and to also move much slower, that things get done in such a way that I am:

1) Not half dead (first of all)
2) Able to be quiet on the inside, i.e., more peace, which is a fruit of the spirit
3) Enjoy the process more
4) Have energy
5) Get it done at a higher level of excellence
6) And getting it done the way God would have it done

I've also learned that to operate in God's grace and His pace, does indeed require a lot more slowing down and waiting. It requires subjecting my flesh which always wants to do this NOW and is always *so* ready to get things done. This can be a painful thing to do, especially when it seems like "everybody else is doing things, why am I still sitting here waiting on my strategy"?

I've learned that it is better to wait on God and walk out my instructions from a place of ease and certainty than it is to jump out in zeal only to crash and burn later. I've learned that God is more interested in my character development and the woman I am becoming in the process, than the actual end result. He is more interested in my motive and intentions behind *why* I am doing something vs. *what* I am doing.

Quite often we are operating in pride with impure motives such as striving to be seen, validated, or to impress others so that people won't see our shame. We don't know how to relax, wait and receive from God or depend on Him.

We are so used to making things happen that we can't even discern if we are led by God or by our own energy. In order to determine whether or not you are operating in your own fleshly zeal and energy, simply note how you feel and the fruit of your activity. Are you in a state of restlessness, lack of peace, confusion, fear, anxiety, or struggle? If so, you are likely operating in your own strength. However, if you are flowing in God and the energy of His grace, there is a peace, a calmness, and an anointing on your efforts. It will still require hard work but there will be a grace on it so the work is also enjoyable.

When we are striving in our flesh, fear steps in and faith steps out. God does too. God can't help us if we are doing all the work.

God is interested in making sure that I have the inner capacity to sustain the outward manifestation of what He will bring into my life before He actually allows the next step to unfold. That is what God does. Catherine Ponder, in her book, The Dynamics of Prayer states that "God waits for order to be established in the current situation of our lives before he allows the next step. Unfortunately, most of us (myself-included) try to jump to the next step, level, realm or position without having adequately gone through the preparatory process that involved the earlier steps. We just want to jump right out there because we think are so ready.

Dr. Cindy Trimm poignantly states in her book, The Prosperous Soul that:

21

"When God blesses you by increasing your business, salary, or influence, it will create more pressure...If He blesses you and your foundation and infrastructure are faulty, blessing you with increase won't feel like a blessing at all...God is not going to bless you with more success than your personal infrastructure can handle – no matter how many lives it may help..."

No matter how great, wonderful, anointed, gifted and talented you are, if your soul has not yet been developed to handle the weight of the calling or mantle on your life, when the pressure of having to maintain and sustain the weight of that level of influence comes, it will overwhelm you and cause burn out.

This is why I am becoming more and more grateful to God for these hidden years. God in His great mercy and kindness would not allow me to get beyond a certain level or a certain point in my ministry or calling. Of course, you could always argue that it is my part of "not getting myself out there, not being consistent, not really hustling and grinding", fear, crutches, excuses and so forth.

All of that has an element of truth. However, as I look back over everything, I realize that for what I am called to do in the area of emotional healing, personal worthiness and relationships, that I really had to go through in a deep and profound way so that I could stand on a platform like this and minister effectively and authentically to people from a place of personal wholeness and freedom.

However, if I did this type of ministry in my flesh and zeal to "get out there", I would live the opposite of what I preached and end up crashed and burned.

Therefore, I die daily by making the intentional choice to become more aware of what is really going on inside by asking myself the following questions. I encourage you to ask these same questions as you evolve into becoming a woman who operates her life from the energy of grace and not her flesh.

1. Where am I striving in my own energy?
2. Am I in peace most of the time or am I in a frenzy, busy and dizzy?
3. What am I doing and why?
4. What am I afraid of?

PRAYER ACTIVATION

"Heavenly Father, I come before you in a place of surrender. I surrender my need for control. I surrender my need to have it all together to impress others. I surrender the need to strive and struggle for what I have been already given. I ask for your grace to come in and flow through me to manifest your will and purpose in my life. I trust you to flow through me in your timing and in your way as I surrender to the call, stay in peace and stay in my lane. Amen."

Chapter 5

WE GO LOW

Pride must die in you, or nothing of heaven can live in you. – **Andrew Murray**

The Bible clearly states in Proverbs 16:18 that pride goes before destruction and a haughty spirit before a fall. Every time I have "fallen" in big ways or in small ways, somewhere along the line – if I do a careful and honest inventory of myself and the sequence of events, thoughts and behaviors that led up to the situation, I am 100% certain that the old subtle, sneaky spirit of pride was in operation.

The thing about pride that is so pervasive and frightening – for lack of better words - is that you can be prideful and not truly aware of it. It slips and dips through so many variations and subtleties of manifestation. For instance, it is perfectly normal and healthy to feel good about your work and to desire to impact more people. It is also a good thing to have a certain amount of drive or ambition in order to "get out there" so that you can be seen to make things happen.

However, this can easily and subtly slide over into a spirit of pride that will run ahead of God to make things happen. It can morph into comparing and competing with others instead of functioning in the spirit of true Kingdom collaboration.

It can show up as needing to be seen, puffed up and validated externally based on works instead of simply being who you are in God. It can turn into the lone ranger syndrome of being unwilling to receive community and connection because of the erroneous (and prideful belief) that you can do it all alone and thus receive all of the credit.

Many friendships have been forfeited and lost because of pride and insecurity. Many things that could have advanced the Kingdom of God and

His purposes for our lives if we listened to the voice of faith and love instead of the voice of accusation, pride and fear that keeps us stuck.

On the other hand, pride can keep you in wrong relationships for too long as well. Pride was one of many factors that kept me in a dead-end relationship for almost seven years waiting to be married. Instead of admitting that I didn't hear from God but rather I heard from my feelings, my flesh and unhealed wounds, I stayed in a clearly toxic situation that was not God's best for me. I wanted God to bless my mess and somehow make it okay so we could get married and serve God according to my fantasy and desires. However, it didn't work that way (which I will be discussing in the next chapter).

Pride can cause us to inadvertently delay breakthroughs, blessings and benefits all because of being too proud to receive the help and wise counsel that holds the key to our next level. Pride shows up as a fear of what other people think so much so that one is willing to go to the extreme of pretending that she has it all together when she does not.

Pride. We must let it go. We have to go low first before we can go high. The Bible says in 1 Peter 5: 6-7 Humble yourselves therefore under the mighty hand of God, that He may exalt you in due time: Casting all your care upon him; for He cares for you. It also says in Hebrews 10:35-36 that we are to cast not away therefore our confidence, which hath great recompense of reward.

Within the context of these two scriptures lies a brief, five step formula for promotion & provision:

1) Humble ourselves before God;
2) Be exalted in due time;
3) Cast our cares;
4) Keep our confidence; and
5) Receive a great reward

Sounds simple and easy, right? But if it were that easy, we wouldn't have the ongoing struggles that we do. Truth be told, we tend to do the opposite of the steps indicated above.

We do the opposite sequence of the above formula:
1) We stay in pride, thus;
2) Disqualify ourselves from being exalted in due season;
3) We keep all of our cares
4) We cast away our confidence.
5) We lose our great reward.

Why? Because of pride and fear. It is a sign of pride to hang onto our issues trying to fix them ourselves instead of admitting that if we knew what we were doing and had it all together like the image we portray, we would have our situation fixed right now. It is pride for me to not humble myself before God's hand and sovereignty.

It takes humility to literally cast our cares on God. It takes humility to maintain patient confidence in knowing that what He started in our life, He will finish if we cooperate.

At the end of the day, we can't come up higher in our purpose and calling unless we come home to God -- i.e., until we humble ourselves under His hand first and foremost.

As you carefully do inventory of your life, I encourage you to pause and reflect on these questions:

REFLECTIVE QUESTIONS

1. What problems or situations have risen in your life that could have been easily resolved if you swallowed your pride and allowed someone in to help you?
2. Are there any cares and concerns that you have right now that you have not truly cast on God but are still holding on emotionally and spiritually trying to figure out a solution in your own mind?
3. What connections and friendships may have been forfeited because of insecurity and pride?
4. On the other side of the above question, what relationships have you stayed in too long and should have ended but your pride (what people will think) kept you in it anyway?

"Heavenly Father, Lord I confess and repent of my pride that is keeping me from walking in and living out my highest and best life. I release to you every care and concern that I am holding onto, trying to fix in my own self-effort. I ask forgiveness for every connection and friendship that I lost as a result of pride and immaturity. I humble myself before you, cast my cares and keep my confidence. In Jesus' Name, Amen."

Chapter 6

GET OUT OF DEAD-END RELATIONSHIPS

Unhealthy ME + Unhealthy HE = Unhealthy WE – **Christine Arylo**

I love this equation. It succinctly sums up the components of what makes a relationship healthy or unhealthy.

Indeed, the only thing that I have control over in this equation is ME.

If I am a healthy ME, I will in turn attract a healthy HE and we can have a Healthy WE.

I can't have a healthy WE, until I first deal with ME.

Often we try furiously and feverishly to create a WE, but we neglect to work on that ME first.

When ME is undeveloped, unhealed and out of alignment with purpose, it will inevitably be unhealthy and of course in the effort to have a WE, Unhealthy ME will attract an unhealthy HE and now we have created an Unhealthy WE.

When we allow ourselves to become energetically, spiritually and emotionally enmeshed and entangled with individuals that we know is not God's best for us, we are unhealthy and have created a toxic soul tie. This not only includes romantic relationships but also other types of relationships.

This may even include family and friends. Sometimes we mean well trying to help, fix and heal them when we need to stay in our own lane and let God do the work. Sometimes we get involved romantically with someone with "potential" out of our "thirst", our need to be seen, loved, or to give love only to find out later that we cannot make a relationship work on someone's "potential" only.

When it comes to matters of the heart, we must connect with individuals who are *already* open, prepared, fruitful, and productive in their purpose.

We must connect with those who are mature and open to authentic, mature love in an effort to have a healthy, mature and loving relationship with them.

For those of us who have done a lot of inner healing, deliverance and mindset renewal work, it is very imperative and necessary that we connect with individuals who:

- Have a genuine and evolving relationship with God as a true believer of Christ
- At our level emotionally, spiritually, & intellectually and know who they are and their purpose.
- Have cooperated with God and done their soul work (i.e., healing from past traumas & romantic soul ties)
- Are expanded enough in their own hearts to be able to receive the love we have to offer
- Have the capacity return love, support and companionship to us at that same level we give.
- Serious and intentional about ongoing personal growth and development.
- Are actively engaged in their life's purpose and calling at the same level or higher.
- At this level, because we have cooperated with the Holy Spirit to heal and order our lives, we cannot waste time with those who:
- Are still not ready for an authentic Kingdom relationship
- Do not want to elevate
- Still want to hide out from purpose or God
- Are in need of counseling and/or deliverance and emotional healing but are avoiding or covering up their pain in dysfunctional ways
- Still struggling to figure out who they are
- Only want surface, shallow or sexual connections when you know you require more.
- Unwilling to invest in or do anything to grow as a person and in their purpose.

They may be wonderful people overall. We may like them, care for them, love them and pray for them. Yet we must realize that in spite of our feelings for them, we must learn to maintain appropriate boundaries because they do not qualify for deep, close or intimate relationship – especially in the area of committed romantic relationships leading to marriage.

We get caught up in other people's lives trying to fix them to avoid our own healing work that needs to be done. We get caught up in romantic partners with potential that we can "pray them through" instead of working on ourselves to attract someone who is already healed and ready. We distract ourselves with a *potential* partner instead of preparing for and waiting for the true *purpose partner*.

We stay in dead-end relationships that hurt us and keep us out of alignment then wonder why it is so painful. We over-give and over extend ourselves in the name of romantic love. Minister Rudeco Roberts states, "Real relationships have real healthy exchange. If there is no real exchange there is no relationship." In other words, if you are giving or putting into a relationship way more than you are actually receiving then you do not have a true relationship. There is no mutual exchange.

Listed below are a few keys signs that you need to cut a relationship and come back home to yourself and to God:

- If you are forfeiting your own personal development and growth as an individual for the sake of being in a relationship or to be married.
- If you are losing who you are in a relationship just to have it, i.e., feeling lost as to who you are as a woman.
- If you are in a co-dependent relationship where you are the strong one and feel obligated to stay because of history and because the other person can't make it without you or vice versa, the other one is strong or has the resources and you feel like you can't make it without them.
- If you are compromising your sexual integrity outside of marriage
- If you are in constant anxiety and confusion because God has already told you "No", yet you remain in the situation
- If the relationship in any way, shape form or fashion diminishes you, distracts you, derails you from God's purposes, and creates destruction or is abusive.

In addition to the above, often we find ourselves in situations where we believe that we have heard from God that a certain individual is the "One." Because of the strong emotions and feelings involved, we believe that we are being Spirit-led when in reality, we are emotion-led, fantasy-led or lust-led. In these instances, we mistake the *intensity* of the emotions we are feeling for true emotional and spiritual *intimacy*. This often leads to repeated cycles of dead-end relationships also.

One of the hallmarks of a healthy relationship is that there is emotional intimacy that goes beyond the initial emotional intensity, i.e., the high and hot feelings in the early stages. Trust me, I know!

Intensity- when it comes to romantic relationships can be defined as a high degree of emotional excitement. High intensity relationships are formed when there is either high risk or high drama or a combination of both. Often present in these emotionally intense relationships is a high level of uncertainty, drama, and fear. These are the types of relationships that can run extremely hot in the beginning but abruptly peter out in a big, fiery crash leaving you speechless and on your knees in confusion and heartbreak the next moment.

On the other hand, relationships that have the hallmark of true intimacy manifest trust, provide a space to be vulnerable with each other, mutual sharing, both partners being understood, a willingness to open your heart without fear. Authentic relationships are those that are willing to take the time to really gather information beyond the initial chemistry, get past our initial "representative" that we all show first, the social media image and really get to know the person (without sexuality leading). These relationships create a foundation for sustainable love and peaceful relationship that can go the distance.

If true intimacy is absent in your current relationship however, but you have high intense sex, dramatic euphoria, and overwhelming feelings of being up and down all of the time, then you are setting yourself up for a big crash. Misinterpreting the euphoria of infatuation and lust for real love can be very costly to your heart and spirit.

Remember --- Lust is not real love. Love always fulfills, enhances, compliments and sustains. Lust drains. Love always *gives* for the benefit of the other person, lust always *takes* for the benefit of self. When we are caught up in intense relationships, we are likely under the throes of lust and infatuation because the primary focus is on how the other person is making us *feel* as to how much they actually are in alignment with who we are as a person and our purpose.

32

When we mistake an entanglement for an authentic, healthy connection we are setting ourselves up for a dead-end relationship. There is a clear distinction between entanglements and connections. Let's look at the definitions:

- *Entanglement:* a complicated or compromising relationship or situation; something that entangles, confuses, or ensnares
- *Connection:* an interdependent association; relation; link; a situation in which two or more things have the same cause, origin, goal, etc.

For purposes of our discussion here, an entanglement is a relationship that compromises who you are as a woman or man of God; that diminishes your perception of your personal worth and value and prohibits you from operating in your God ordained purpose. An entanglement brings confusion, chaos, emotional stress and anxiety. It is a true dead-end situation.

An authentic, healthy connection, on the other hand, is when two separate, yet complete growing individuals come together to add value, enhance and support each other's lives. Healthy connection brings security and sustainability over time that creates a foundation for both individuals to maximize their God-give purpose under the umbrella of mutual companionship and true intimacy. It is what true love looks like.

If you are in any type of situation that is not in alignment with a healthy, authentic connection that gives life --- It's time to cut it and come back home!

REFLECTIVE QUESTIONS

1. If you are in a relationship right now, take a moment to evaluate if this person is in alignment with your purpose.
2. What are you doing now to work on cultivating the Healthy ME so that you can attract a Healthy HE?
3. As you look back over your relationship history, think back to the times where you were caught up in entanglements instead of true relationships? Are there any recurring patterns in these relationships?

"Heavenly Father, I ask that you come in right now and reveal to me the true nature of my romantic relationships both past and present. Lord show me the lessons that my soul needed to learn about myself. Empower me to walk with you in the power of the Holy Spirit to cultivate a Healthy ME. Empower me to cut the ties to unhealthy and toxic connections and deepen my capacity to discern the counterfeits from the truly called ones. In Jesus' Name, Amen."

Chapter 7

DOES IT REALLY MATTER?

You see, in the final analysis, it is between you and God; It was never between you and them anyway.

– Mother Theresa

*I*n looking back over your life, especially the last few experiences where you have felt offended, wounded, or hurt. Those times where someone you admired and loved fell short of your expectations. Perhaps there was some sort of misunderstanding. Perhaps they had a very bad day. Or maybe both of your insecurities came out and were exposed and you projected on one another. Then after that you slowly drifted apart. Yet you know you love them, but somehow it didn't turn into the close friendship, relationship or partnership that you thought you were going to have with them.

It hurts. The interesting thing is that the higher you elevate and start to move in God's will and purpose for your life, true and genuine friends become few and far between. It's because there are fewer and fewer people with the same mindset that you have. The sad reality is that not a lot of people function at a very high level of productivity and personal purpose. If you are one of those few people, it's best to get used to that fact now and simply focus on cultivating a few high-quality relationships.

In reflecting upon earlier disappointing relationships and situations, carefully ponder this question:

Will what I am struggling with, brooding and stewing over about what happened in this relationship or situation really matter 200 years from now? A year from now? Will I remember this? Will anyone else remember this? Is it really that important?

This is especially true when it comes to other people – their opinions, who's mad at you, who likes you, who said/did what, etc. If, in the grand scheme of your life and purpose, you determine that it does not really matter in the long view, then why is it dominating your mind in the short-term view?

We are reminded in Colossians 3:2 (AMP) to "Set our minds and keep them set on things above (the higher things), not on things of the earth. Simply put, this means to elevate your mind to think the way God thinks, to see and function at a higher level. This requires not allowing yourself to get overly bogged down in your earthly, fluctuating circumstances as if they are permanent and forever. Eternal things are forever. Your earthly circumstances are not.

If you have made the determination that what you are struggling with doesn't matter in the long-term grand scheme of things, then it means you must let it go.

Let go of petty offenses, slights, little hurts, criticisms, vain imaginations faster and faster. There is a brief window of less than two minutes or so when you first hear, see or perceive of a situation that hurts and offends you. Within that instance is the time frame that you must decide.

In that moment, is when you can:

1) Decide to let it pass;
2) Choose not to say anything yet or until you have had time to process (never speak out of emotions);
3) Pray within yourself in the moment;
4) Release it quick, and;
5) If necessary, journal later
6) If you decide something needs to be said; do it only with wisdom, consideration, prayer and coming from a place of love and not defense.

Regardless of whatever course of action you decide to take in your situation, whatever you do, refuse to rehash and ruminate about the situation or the person for hours in your mind and talk about it to ten different people. When we stop the hitting the mental rewind and replay buttons in our head, it lessens the pain.

At the end of the day, we really must grow up.

We must mature to the point where we stop taking other people's actions, words, perceptions, thoughts, behaviors so incredibly personal. It really is about their belief system, worldview and how they perceive themselves and you. Their perception of you and your thoughts, words, and behaviors are not necessarily true.

Therefore, we don't have to be so offended and take it so personal. We can choose not to receive or believe the negative and it if it's true, we are secure and whole enough (because we have come home to God and ourselves and know that we are loved and accepted by Him) that we can receive wise and constructive criticism without getting "in our feelings."

Another way in which we can maintain healthy boundaries in our relationships with others is to stay in our lanes emotionally and mentally. In other words, be very careful to avoid getting enmeshed and entangled in other people's business and affairs that you avoid dealing with your own issues.

Examples of this would include the mother who smothers her sons and won't give them space because she doesn't have her own life. Or the person who can't do anything, make any decisions and think for themselves without the input of an overly intrusive friend or family member who is all up in their business.

This is known as enmeshment or entanglement. These are the situations where families and friends are overly involved in the details of each other's lives in an unhealthy and dysfunctional way.

I heard this quote and it sums it up so well. Imagine your life being a car and you are driving on the freeway of life:

✗ *When you try to drive in someone else's lane, you will wreck.*
When you try to navigate in God's lane you get lost.
When you stay in our own lane, you have peace.

If I try to get involved in someone else's journey at the expense of my own soul development, i.e., trying to help, fix, heal and deliver them while I am still struggling and unaware of my own issues, I will most certainly crash and cause both myself and the other person pain.

If I try to control and manipulate things out of fear or try to figure things out and make things happen on my own, I am now getting in God's lane and since God's ways are higher than my ways and His thoughts my thoughts according to Isaiah 55:11 I most certainly will get lost. I don't have the knowledge or GPS system of God to know where I am going in His lane. Confusion, chaos and calamity is sure to result.

However, the moment I make an intentional choice to bloom where I am planted and stay in my own lane on the highway of life, I will most certainly have peace.

✗ If you want peace over pain, stay in your lane!

REFLECTIVE QUESTIONS

1. Think over your friendships and connections over the past few years. Have they started to shift and drift once you became serious and intentional about your walk with God and your purpose?
2. Looking over your interactions in relationships in hindsight, can you see where it is possible that both of you may have projected insecurities and fears on each other?
3. Can you think of a situation where you tried to fix or help someone else at the expense of your own healing and growth? How did this work out?

PRAYER ACTIVATION

"Heavenly father, I repent of the situations in which I allowed my insecurities, pride and fear to cause me to project and push my issues on someone that you sent in my life to help me. Lord, help me continue to develop and deepen as the Woman of God you have called me to be. Let me grow into becoming the kind of person that naturally attracts the right caliber of people and connections for this new dimension that I am walking into. I release the need to fix, heal and deliver people. Help me to use that energy to heal and order my own life. In Jesus' name, Amen."

PART 2

THE NEXT DIMENSION

Chapter 8

ACTIVATING THE SPIRIT OF COMPLETION

Loose ends.
Unfinished business.
Things left hanging
Lingering, longstanding unresolved issues.
Paperwork undone.
Lack of private order.

*A*s long as we have the above floating around in the underbelly and backgrounds of our lives, there will always be a level of "drag" or "resistance" every time we attempt to move forward in life and purpose.

No one is immune. As a matter of fact, the busier you are, the more influence and impact you are making, the greater the proclivity to generate more loose ends, unfinished business and general disorder.

Why? Because you are moving so fast and getting so much done, that you don't have time to clean up emotionally, physically and spiritually as you go on to the next thing. Often we are moving so fast that we don't allow for adequate transition space between the various seasons and times of life.

I'll be the first to raise my hand here. I am the one that typically moves so fast that I don't have time to clean as I go, I get tired, things pile up and never get fully resolved. If I am not careful, everything will eventually come to a head and crash at the most inopportune time. The funny thing is, I am aware of it, but often am too weary to get it done. That is another key part as well. Maintaining your strength and stamina to clean and order your life as you move without fatigue is critical.

I always see in hindsight how something could have been prevented or I could have mitigated from further damage had I taken a few extra moments or perhaps an hour or day or two, just to get it done or deal with it.

However, on the opposite end of the spectrum are those who never move at all, but are keenly aware of their loose ends, unfinished business and personal disorder and stay stuck in powerlessness, shame and fear, thus never getting things done. At one point in my journey, I was stuck here also, but by my very nature it was difficult to stay here. Even at this point, I would do little things to keep the needle pointing and shifting towards some type of progress. The key here is taking baby steps even in the midst of imperfection and disorder, still cleaning and ordering as you move.

In both situations – you move quickly or you don't move at all, resistance and drag create untimely delay, distraction and destruction if not dealt with appropriately. For those of us who are elevating and moving forward, we must be very intentional to slow down and operate at the pace of grace so that we clean and handle our business as we go instead of letting it pile up. For those of us who get stuck in the unfinished business, we must be very intentional to not let our issues bog us down and immobilize us from doing what God called us to do.

The secret is activating the Spirit of Completion.

When we fail to bring situations, events, physical things (such as paperwork and loose-ends) to completion, it is a representation of still hanging on to the past. It is a representation of old things from an old season that we are dragging into the present season because it is still yet incomplete business.

This not only includes the items listed above in the beginning of this chapter, but it also includes relationships that need to end or have some type of closure. It also represents emotional ties and struggles that need to end.

I heard this quote somewhere, "You can't bring old thoughts into a new season." That is basically the essence of what unfinished business is.

However, the Spirit of Completion is something else altogether. It is not so much as the Spirit of Completion, but rather the rhythm of completion. The rhythm of completion occurs when we finish what we start. It occurs when we bring a situation, a process, a project, a relationship from one stage to the next in a timely fashion.

Every time we engage in the rhythm of completion, we increase in confidence and stamina.

In Ecclesiastes 7:8 we read, that better is the ending of a thing than the beginning and the patient in spirit is better than the proud in spirit. Completion brings confidence. Always.

Every time you start something – a God idea project, plan, business, ministry but don't bring it to completion, it chips away at your self-esteem. There is nothing worse than breaking your promise to yourself. But we honor ourselves and God when (with His help) we bring things through to completion. There is a big difference between those who start many projects with great excitement and gusto from those who finish a few and patiently complete them well.

By way of example, imagine in your minds' eye a mother cat who has given birth to twelve kittens. However, she only has ten nipples to feed them. What do you think will happen to two of the kitties? Because she lacks personal capacity or space to feed all her kittens, there will be at least two "runts or the litter" or worse yet, two of the kittens will likely die of malnutrition.

Now look at the person who is a "professional starter". This person always has many, many ideas and tries to start them all but due to the fact that they lack personal bandwidth and capacity, they are unable to finish or complete them all. Eventually, very little or few of them actually come to full manifestation in excellence.

It takes faith, focus, diligence and the ability to begin with the end in mind. It takes discipline to decide every single day to up-level and elevate which often requires delayed gratification and the ability to say no to certain things.

Dr. Cindy Trimm states, "Freedom is the ability to say no, when yes is more convenient." More often than not, it is much easier to say yes to a distraction, yes to procrastination than it is to say yes to completing that book project or ministry idea.

A huge part of coming home to yourself and coming up higher is simply completing or finishing your business be it personal or otherwise that you have started. It is estimated that roughly 2% of people actually finish what they start. These individuals in the 2% group tend to operate at a different elevation or atmosphere mentally because as indicated, they have a different spirit.

When we are driven to distraction or stuck in procrastination we are unable to complete anything. The key to operating in the consistency or rhythm of completion is to look at the root cause of distraction and procrastination – fear.

It is fear of man – i.e., "what will the infamous *they* think?" about our project, idea, book or whatever it is. It is the fear of being vulnerable to the criticism of others when you put yourself out there and step into the unknown. The key question to ask here is not what they think about you, but what will YOU think about you when you fail to complete your God-given assignment?

Remember, every time you complete something your self-esteem and your confidence increases. Every time you finish what you start, your relationship with yourself grows stronger. Why? Because you have proven to be trustworthy within yourself.

Think about it. How do you feel when someone repeatedly says that they are going to call or text you, but they never do? How do you feel when someone fails to show up when they said they would? What does it feel like when someone makes promises to you or agrees to do X, Y & Z but suddenly you never hear from them?

Now, take that same feeling and apply it to yourself. You make sincere and repeated intentions, promises, resolutions, prayers, goals to accomplish certain things and then you fail to show up.

If you can't trust yourself to follow through, how can you be trusted? If I cannot be faithful with the little things for my own self development, how can God trust me with much? (Luke 16:10) If I can't trust myself, how can I trust other people, much less God?

However, when I start becoming a consistent starter *and* finisher, I have now shown myself to be trustworthy and faithful. I have positioned myself to be blessed and to walk in greater degrees of confidence. As confidence arises, so does peace, clarity and an overall sense of greater personal worthiness.

I have one very deep question to ask you.

What are you waiting for?

Whatever God has called you to do – do it *now*. Take the initial baby steps. Start moving in the direction of your assignment in this season. *Now* is the accepted time. *Now* is the day of salvation! (2 Cor. 6:2). Christ is the author and the finisher of our faith (Heb 12:2). He has begun a good work in you and will complete it, if you cooperate. (Phil 1:6)

REFLECTIVE QUESTIONS

1. As you look over your life, can you identify certain seasons where you were overwhelmed, and things piled up on you – emotionally, physically, mentally and in your environment? How did you get back on track?
2. Take a few moments and write down all of your personal unfinished business that is causing you to delay moving forward in your purpose. What baby steps can you take today to point the needle forward?
3. Imagine what it would feel like to transition from the state of not finishing to actually moving in the Spirit of Completion? How does this boost your self-esteem?

PRAYER ACTIVATION

"Heavenly Father, I repent for allowing the distraction and overwhelm of my life to keep me from fulfilling my purpose. Reveal to me any hidden emotional and spiritual unfinished business. Help me to embrace the truth that I can do all things in Christ who strengthens me. (Phil 4:13). I thank you in advance for the victory that I will enjoy as I walk daily in completing my God ordained assignment in this season of my life. In Jesus' name, Amen."

Chapter 9

WE WALK BY FAITH & VISION, NOT FEELINGS & SIGHT

The only thing worse than being blind is having sight and no vision. – **Hellen Keller**

*W*e walk by faith and not by sight (2 Cor 5:7). Might I add we do not walk by how we feel from moment to moment. Our feelings can go up and down and all over the place on a moment's notice. Major and minor life decisions cannot be made on a whim based on our feelings at the moment. Decisions must be made in alignment with God's purpose for our lives not based on short-sighted feelings.

Our purpose is not predicated upon our circumstances, insecurities, inadequacies or mistakes. Our purpose is based on the truth of God's word --- who He says we are in Him now that our lives have been redeemed. Feelings can lie and feelings can deceive. They are meant to be felt and acknowledged, but not acted upon without proper thought and checking in with God through prayer.

Having a clear and distinct vision of your life and operating from that vision as opposed to what you see in your natural sight or current set of circumstances is crucial.

Without vision, you will rely on your natural sight and instead of coming up higher, you will inevitably drop down lower to match your circumstances.

Where your mind goes your body follows. Your mouth and speech will begin to align with what you don't want for your life instead of God's vision. To come up higher requires having a vision and lining up your actions and words to reflect the vision God has for you.

Vision is defined as the ability to think about or plan the future with imagination or wisdom. Vision naturally elevates you. Why does vision elevate us? Vision elevates because it takes us into a higher realm of reality than the one we currently exist in. Vision elevates us because it takes us into the realm of God. Vision elevates us because it stretches our faith to believe for something that we are not presently experiencing in our day-to-day reality, but gives us hope for that which is sure to come.

Take into consideration the following quote form P.K. Bernard:

"A man without a vision is a man without a future. A man without a future will always return to his past."

When we wander aimlessly through life without a clear sense of direction, purpose and vision, we will inevitably fall back to our comfort zone or we will revert back to the past. No substantial progress in your God ordained purpose for your life will be made without having a vision for it.

I might add here, that the vision does not have to be fully perfected. You will not know everything. The notion that your vision must be perfectly laid out, with every detail for everything that is going to happen already considered is unrealistic. The key element to walking by faith and not by sight is the factor of the unknown -- -the God Factor.

Trying to have a perfect, flawless vision or idea in your head about how you think your life purpose is supposed to unfold is a surefire recipe for disappointment, disillusionment and despair.

The vision must have enough detail, be clear enough and strong enough to give you something to hope for and work towards in terms of your thoughts, words, behaviors, your lifestyle lining up to meet it, but it cannot be so detailed and perfected that it leaves no room for God to be involved. In other words, we must surrender and relinquish control back to God for the best and optimal chance that His vision for our lives would come to pass in His timing and in His way.

This again, is where we tend to fall apart.

The moment things start going awry. When circumstances and distractions scream and the vision and purpose God has spoken over your life becomes a tiny whisper. It is in those moments that your natural sight overwhelms your God-ordained vision and your faith is being tested to not only stand in the evil day, but to remain steadfast without wavering. This is when we forget that we walk by faith and not by sight or feelings, but instead we start walking by what we see and what we feel.

48

The net result of walking, talking and acting by what we see and feel in the natural and in the moment, is usually almost always entirely unsupportive and detrimental to God's vision and our purpose. The result of letting our feelings and what we see in the natural overrule and override what the God given vision says is that we will get more of the same disappointments and struggles in our lives. Remember, what you focus on grows.

VISION FLOWS FROM THE HEART

The state of your heart determines the visibility and sustainability of your vision. We find in scripture that:

1) Out of the heart flows the issues of our lives;
2) The spiritual eyes of our heart must be enlightened so that we can know and understand the hope of our calling; and
3) Our spiritual eyes of the heart are the lamp of our whole bodies, i.e., if our eyes are sound or healthy, we will walk in light, but if our spiritual eyes are unhealthy, we will be in perpetual darkness. (Proverbs 4:23, Ephesians 1:18 and Matthew 6:22-23)

Clearly, the state of our hearts affect our capacity and ability to have spiritual vision or insight into the will of God for our lives. Every issue of our life, i.e., the thoughts we think, our emotions, reactions, biases, proclivities, all of our decisions come from our hearts.

Out of the abundance of the heart, the mouth speaks (Matt. 12:34). Because we are speaking spirits that bring forth creation and manifestation when we speak (whether or not we are aware of it, doesn't diminish this fact), we begin to set in motion with our speech and concurrent actions the course of our destiny and the issues of our life.

Without acute and keen awareness of what is going on in our hearts and what we are speaking forth out of our mouths, we could wreak significant damage in our lives and those around us thereby hindering the vision of God for our lives or even sometimes aborting it all together.

The goal for all of us who believe is to have the eyes of our hearts perpetually enlightened so that we can know the hope of our calling in God – i.e. the vision.

When the eyes of our heart are dark or unhealthy with unconfessed sin and emotional wounding, we will walk in darkness and unable to see the vision for our lives, much less execute with any degree of clarity and alignment with God.

We will walk around aimlessly - speaking and doing things that are in direct opposition to what God said all because we are in the dark when it comes to his vision and purpose for our lives.

Thus, the key to understanding and walking in God's vision for your life begins and ends with the heart. Without a clear and sound heart, you will walk according to unregulated thoughts and feelings stemming from your natural circumstances as opposed to the light and clarity that comes when we turn the eyes of our hearts toward God.

Coming back full circle, to have a heart ready for vision means first receiving salvation, working out your own soul salvation (which means your personal healing and deliverance process as you renew your mind) and then making the intentional choice to walk by faith instead of natural sight and feelings.

It's a heart thing.

REFLECTIVE QUESTIONS

1. As you look over your life, think of the times where you allowed your circumstances and feelings to take over and acted out of your emotions. What was the end result and what did you learn about yourself?
2. Think about the vision God has placed in your heart. Have you been waiting for all of the full details and to have everything figured out before moving forward? What steps are you going to take now to move forward?
3. Clarity of heart is crucial.to manifesting God's vision for your life. Take the time to do a heart check to see if there are any unhealed wounds that are blocking clarity of vision.

PRAYER ACTIVATION

"Heavenly Father, thank you for your grace and patience with me in the journey of manifesting your vision for my life. I repent of the times where I fell apart emotionally when I saw my circumstances and walked by sight instead of faith. Create in me a clean heart and renew a right spirit so that I can clearly see the vision you have for me. Give me the strength and courage to continue to move forward despite what my feelings and circumstances may dictate. In Jesus' name, Amen."

Chapter 10

THE SMALL DECISIONS TURN
THE WHEELS OF DESTINY

Life is the sum of all your choices. – **Albert Camus**

*I*t's the little small things that you have done all year long last year that got you to where you are this exact moment in time. The secret to the good things that happened so far this year and yes, the challenges too can be found in your daily thoughts, daily habits, the words you spoke, and how you chose to act consistently over time.

Your future outcomes for any area of your life can be predicted by observing your behaviors and habits starting from the smallest thing that you do on autopilot without even thinking to the larger decisions (which are a series of smaller ones) over time.

Every major thing in your life began with a thought that led to feelings which in turn initiated into a series of decisions. That relationship. Agreeing to say yes. Agreeing to sleep with that person. Agreeing to sign that contract. Saying yes when you should have said no. Saying no when you should have said yes. Sending that email. Responding to that inbox message on Facebook or Instagram. All of it.

In his book, Divine Direction, Craig Groeschel states "Like falling dominoes, even our smallest decisions sometimes cascade into consequences we never could have seen coming...the decisions we make today determine the stories we tell tomorrow." Can you think back on situations in your life in which you made a simple small decision and things manifested that you never even imagined? Was it for your good or did it turn out less than favorable? The kicker is what did you learn from it? Remember what you don't learn from and extract wisdom from, will come back around again until you get the lesson!

53

The other side to this is, if you really want to come up higher in every area of your life you must master the art of being consistent with the small daily actions that lead to victory. The Bible states in Zechariah 4:10, Do not despise these small beginnings, for the Lord rejoices to see the work begin --- and a few scriptures before that we are reminded in the 6th verse - Not by might, nor by power, but by My Spirit. So we are not to be discouraged when we are still struggling to take our daily baby steps but to rely and depend upon the Spirit of God – His strength and power.

We often struggle in our own strength to stay the course when things look tiny and small. Sometimes it is a battle to consistently make the small daily decisions that no one sees but you and God. That is where the victory is won. This is where the rubber meets the road. Groeshel goes on to state, "It's the small choices no one sees that result in the big impact everyone wants..."

Osazee Thompson in his book, Precision Purpose states that "Consistency is the key to performance." In other words, consistency is the capacity to keep doing what is right when no one is looking and when it appears that nothing is happening. Consistency is the ability to show up with the right set of thoughts which drive our feelings and ultimately our subsequent actions.

Let's be consistent to show up and be faithful when the results look dismal or non-existent. Let's not be weary in the well doing. We will reap if we faint not.

Fainting will occur when we let our minds dwell on the past and in our circumstances (go back to Chapter 8: We Walk by Faith and Vision). Fainting will occur when we allow our negative feelings to run the show. Fainting will also occur when we allow guilt and condemnation to come along side of us and put voices in our heads every time we mess up.

We faint because we don't feel worthy and tend to believe that we've already messed up and what is the use in trying and so forth. Because we are human we will fall short. The key to when you fall short is to not faint, but to slow down, catch your breath, repent, receive forgiveness, forgive yourself and get back into the ring again and show up consistently.

Case in point, I have consistently established the daily practice of rising early in the morning to pray, praise and worship, read the bible or study a bible-based book in a specific subject matter for over fifteen years now. This was a hard-won victory. A fellow sister in Christ asked me to be one of the devotion leaders on a daily early morning prayer call starting at 5:30 am. I was asked to speak a word of inspiration to the ladies on the call. I said yes, I was already up at that time anyway.

Well on one particular call, I was asked to speak from my other book, Get Out of That Dead End Relationship NOW. Unbeknownst to me, a lady was on the line (whom I did not know) and happened to be in the process of planning a Singles Conference and heard me speak. Within thirty minutes of the call ending, she reached out to me and asked if I'd speak at her conference – *suddenly*. From the same morning call, came forth an in-person speaking engagement. It all began with a simple decision to say yes, to do the devotion and pray.

I wasn't striving to get speaking engagements. I wasn't trying to do anything. I simply said yes to help others and was obedient. This one small decision, expanded my life in ways I never imagined. This one "yes" had a domino effect that never crossed my mind when I agreed to do the call. This is the power of making the small, but right decision to show up and be obedient.

Take a moment and think about people you currently admire. It may appear that out of nowhere they became famous overnight. Realize that this is truly an *appearance*. Rest assured that there were many seemingly *tiny, right* decisions that piled up over time, created momentum and coalesced into what you see today.

It is a result of consistent needlepoint shifts over the course of years that have the cumulative effect of *appearing* to happen all at once.

1. What about you? What daily small steps that you could be taking right now that could change the trajectory of your life?
2. Be not weary in well doing for in due season, you will reap if you faint not (Gal. 6:9). Doing the right thing every day when no one is looking and when it seems like nothing is happening is difficult. Can you recall any times where you gave up and realized later that if you stayed the course, you would've had your breakthrough? What did you learn from this situation?
3. Consistency is key. What are some areas that you know God is calling you to be more consistent in when it comes to your purpose, your relationships and your personal growth?

PRAYER ACTIVATION

"Heavenly Father, I thank you for the season of small beginnings. Help me to endure the seasons where it appears that nothing is happening, no one sees me and there seems to be no reward for my effort. Strengthen me to continue to make the small, daily wise decisions that will lead me to prosper in your will for my life. Give me an eternal perspective on my daily decision making so that I make decisions that impact my destiny in a way that glorifies and honors you. In Jesus' name, Amen."

Chapter 11

PRAISE & WORSHIP: THE FREQUENCY OF HEAVEN

I will bless the Lord at all times: his praise shall continually be in my mouth.

-Ps. 34:1

*O*n the road to coming up higher, there will inevitably be pain points. There will be moments of deep frustration. We are not to gloss over our pain, numb it, and pretend it does not exist. In John 4:24 we read that God is spirit and that we must worship Him in spirit and in truth. Therefore, we don't minimize what we are going through, but we speak truthfully and pour out to God and in the midst of it find a way to praise him anyhow. It is in the crying out to God that we receive relief. We do not receive help and comfort through:

1) Endless scrolling through social media
2) Staying over busy with mindless activities
3) Getting caught up in other people's business to prevent from dealing with your own issues.
4) Being fixated on your significant other/boyfriend/husband/fiancé, and the relationship to the expense of what is really going on in your own head and heart
5) Overeating, overdrinking, over sexing, or over spiritualizing

Instead of the above, we receive strength for the journey by really getting real with yourself, facing the pain and making a conscious choice to praise and worship God. Why is this so critical to coming up higher as a woman? Because genuine heartfelt praise *always* elevates. Gratitude and a spirit of thanksgiving will change your atmosphere. You can't come up higher with a dead, negative, or depressed atmosphere. God doesn't operate in that realm! He is the Spirit of Peace, Love and Joy. He is not the spirit of depression, anger, sadness and frustration.

We are entitled to acknowledge those negative emotions. We are to acknowledge and sit in them long enough to identify and observe what is going on inside of us, but we are not to linger in it forever. Why? Our mindsets, our spirits, our emotions must be in alignment with the frequency and the atmosphere of heaven to receive heaven's results.

If I claim that I want a manifestation and miracle, a move of God to bring me to a higher level, then I must first already be at and maintain my ground emotionally, spiritually and mentally at that level *first* before I can experience the manifestation of the next level in my outward natural circumstances. Prayer, praise and worship helps to establish the environment of heaven in your mind and heart before it ever begins to manifest outwardly in your circumstances.

In other words, for my natural circumstances to come up higher or rise to a new level, I must first come up higher in my inner world -- my thought life, emotions and spirit. My spiritual frequency (or vibration as some call it) needs to come up higher to God's frequency – of light, love, power, faith and goodness. I can't come up higher if I allow my emotions, thoughts and spirit to always be tethered down by my circumstances. I can't come up higher if my feelings are at the whim of what is going on around me.

If I allow my fluctuating feelings to run the show, I can be taken captive at any time by the enemy of my soul because of my own instability. Learning how to thank God and praise Him in the midst of trying circumstances has a stabilizing and maturing effect on our souls.

We develop inner fortitude, greater depth and capacity to the extent we can allow God to work in us during trying times and still be able to maintain a praise and spirit of thanksgiving.

In James 1: 3-4 (AMP), we are encouraged to:

Consider it nothing but joy, my [b]brothers and sisters, whenever you fall into various trials. Be assured that the testing of your faith [through experience] produces endurance [leading to spiritual maturity, and inner peace]. And let endurance have its perfect result and do a thorough work, so that you may be perfect and completely developed [in your faith], lacking in nothing.

To contemplate the idea of having joy whenever I "fall into" various situations that are trying is not an easy feat. The only way to do this is through the power of God and making the intentional choice to turn your mind towards Him while things are going on all around you that could cause you to give up and quit.

Our scripture at the beginning of this chapter – Psalm 34:1 summarizes it perfectly. In this scripture the psalmist states, I will bless the Lord at all times and His praise shall continually be in my mouth. Note two key words: *all* and *continually.*

This does not leave room for speculation as to how often we are to bless and praise God. He clearly states all times and continually. This implies that whatever the situation is (again we are not avoiding it or living in denial) but we are making the conscious decision to elevate our mindset to meet God in the midst of our situations.

In order to maintain soul level stability, praise and worship is paramount. Worshiping and praising God helps to recalibrate our soul to the frequency of heaven. Worshiping and praising God elevates us to where God is away from the fret and fever of what is going on around us. Worship and praise is a true mind regulator.

Last, but definitely not least is the fact that praise and worship is a very critical weapon of spiritual warfare. The enemy of our souls cannot operate around us when we have taken over the atmosphere around us and within us with the spirit of praise and thanksgiving. He cannot function in an environment where words of praise, worship and thanksgiving to God are going on.

We learn in 2 Cor. 10:4 that the weapons of our warfare are not physical but are mighty through God for the pulling down of strongholds. Strongholds are any area of your life – emotions, thought process, belief system or mindset that exalts itself against the knowledge of the known will of God and His word.

Therefore, it stands to reason that if the enemy is attempting to come against your mind with anxious, vexing, contrary and negative thoughts, or if he is using the people or circumstances around you to create strife or confusion then it is a perfect time to utilize the weapon of praise and worship. If there is any level of unusual activity in your life that points to the handiwork of satan, rest assured that with prayer, praise and worship you will be able to stop it.

We also can stand on the promise in Isaiah 26:3 that if we keep our mind on God, He will keep us in peace. Part of the beauty and the practicality of praise and worship is that it is an excellent way to keep our mind on God. By focusing on the problem solver rather than our problem, not what the devil is doing, not what other people have said, not on this or that – but God....we will have peace.

A peaceful mind is a powerful mind. A peaceful mind is one that is tuned into the frequency of God and can receive heaven's results.

REFLECTIVE QUESTIONS

1. What are you doing to maintain the frequency of heaven in your heart and life?
2. When the onslaught of thoughts rush through your mind, what is your method of managing it and how is it working for you?
3. As you reflect over your life, can you identify the typical situations, triggers and people that cause you to lose your peace? What can you do to prevent or prepare for this when you know it is coming?

PRAYER ACTIVATION

"Heavenly Father, in your presence is fullness of joy (Ps. 16:11). When I am going through the battles and trials of life, help me to remember to tap into my spiritual strength and power to change the atmosphere by praising and worshiping you. Let me not keep my mouth shut in fear but enable me to fully engage in the spiritual battle with the armor you have given me. As I endure, help me to keep my mind focused on you knowing that the battle is not mine, but yours (2 Chron. 20:15). In Jesus' name, Amen."

Chapter 12

SURRENDER TO THE SEASON.
WHAT YOU RESIST PERSISTS

Where focus goes, energy flows. – **Tony Robbins**

*W*hatever situation currently going on in my life that is not going my way after I have done all I know to do, if I resist and fixate on it in my mind and emotions with negativity, the situation will continue to persist. In other words, the more I resist, the worse I will feel. The more I focus on it, the bigger the situation becomes.

Imagine this scenario. You are driving along in your car and you hit a deep patch of mud and your tires get stuck. You keep hitting the accelerator in an attempt to drive out of the mud, but alas, the wheels become even more stuck in the mud as they continue to spin, going deeper and deeper into the mud.

Well, it is the same way with us. When we keep trying to force an outcome or when we resist the situation because it is not lining up into the perfect answer or solution according to our limited view, we dig a deeper hole and get stuck emotionally and mentally. As a matter of fact, Carl Jung said not only does it (the problem) persist it *grows* in size.

When we attach our happiness to a specific person's actions or words or to a certain outcome, we give away our power. For instance, if they didn't call back, show up, or reply to our text immediately now suddenly, we are feeling "some kind of way." Or if the relationship, the business idea or the ministry didn't pan out the way we imagined or prayed it would and now we are overcome with feelings of not being enough or we take it very personal.

We are losing our personal power that God gave us when we attach or enslave ourselves to certain things happening a certain way within a certain time frame.

Whenever we refuse to surrender to God's timing and His way, but instead choose to resist in negativity, force or enslave ourselves to certain outcomes, we do the following:

- Invite the spirit of desperation and fear
- Repel faith and grace
- Get into works of flesh, pride & ego
- Become impatient and get into a spirit of haste or rush
- Start forcing an outcome according to preconceived notion or fantasy
- Create bigger problems and more delay
- Breed rigidity to a certain way
- Don't allow for creativity and God to move.

Living like this reflects a desperate need to control. The reality is that we cannot control the divine process of manifestation. When we attempt to control situations, people and processes that can only be handled by God, we place ourselves in the very insecure and unstable position of having our peace being dictated based upon whether certain events occur or whether certain people do/say/perform/behave a certain way. This is a very emotionally unstable way to live.

We also lose peace and create internal instability when we are in state of attachment to God doing things a certain way – according to the vision or fantasy in our heads. In this case, what we are really trying to do is know the unknown and demand that we know everything upfront, i.e., trying to be God.

The key is surrender.

Surrender is not a bad word. It is simply releasing outcomes to God. When you have been obedient to do what you know to do and then you release it to God, that is true surrender. When we trust God we are in essence saying, "God either way this happens or unfolds, I know it is working for my good." According to Romans 8:28 all things are truly working together for good. The key to surrender is to fall back, chill and trust.

Remember, every time panic, fear, and disempowerment step in, faith has stepped out! You know you are going too far into your own mind trying to figure, fixate and force something when you find yourself succumbing to these negative emotions. You know you have gone too far when you are overthinking, getting in other people's lanes and losing your peace.

When we fall back, chill and trust we create space for grace and give God an opportunity to flow into the situation.

However, when we get into force, figuring, and fixating we block up the path to clarity and answers with our own inner workings and negativity! Our fears and resistance create blocks. Faith and release creates flow.

This is the state that allows life to flow. Life for the believer is Christ Himself who is the Way, the Truth and the Life. (John: 14:6)

Life (Christ) doesn't flow into your situation from a place of fear, resistance and panic. Life flows from a place of acceptance, faith and peace. Then from this emotional and mental place and state, your environment is now conducive to a positive change. This is also known as surrender.

This is the process of releasing a situation to God and allowing things to unfold naturally as you remain steadfast in faith. Focus, don't force, Flow don't fixate. Detach don't digress back to the old way of fearful thinking.

Know that it is not by your human power nor by might that anything happens in your life, but it is only by God's Spirit that things begin to move (Zech 4:6). With that said, your main course of action in terms of your inner world and attitude is to simply be still and to know that He is God (Ps. 46:10). In other words, you will take the necessary steps that are orderly as you are led by God to do in terms of actual action, however, on the inside you intentionally choose to maintain a posture of inner stillness.

Why is this so important to coming up higher --- Because your fixation and rigidity on how you want things to unfold and happen is what is keeping you down. The moment you let go of how you think things should unfold is the moment things begin to manifest and you begin to rise and come up and out to a new level --- to come up means to fall back, chill and trust the process!! No more white knuckling and hanging on for dear life. Let. It. Go.!!

REFLECTIVE QUESTIONS

1. In your journey, have you found it difficult to practice letting go emotionally and mentally of a situation? Think about a current situation in your life right now and begin to release it to God.
2. What areas of your life appear to be shaky and uncertain? Remember that we walk by faith and not by sight. What is God teaching you in this process?
3. Could there be an old story, trigger or unhealed area of the heart that God is revealing to you that needs to be released in this situation? What do you believe needs to be healed?

PRAYER ACTIVATION

"Heavenly, I release my rigidity. Letting go allows You to flow in my situation. I understand that being resistant and fixating, I am keeping my problems with me. I relinquish my false sense of control and surrender to your timing. Today I intentionally chose to let go, chill & trust the process. In Jesus' Name, Amen."

Chapter 13

WE MOVE FROM GLORY TO GLORY

And we all, with unveiled faces reflecting the glory of the Lord, are being transformed into the same image from one degree of glory to another, which is from the Lord, who is the Spirit.

-2 Corinthians 3:18 (NET)

*O*ne of the most foundational truths of life is this -- we do not change our thinking, emotional or relational patterns all in one fell swoop. We do not come up higher all at once. Typically speaking, profound changes in the mind, emotions and spirit occur gradually over time with great intentionality and consistency to "do the work". We literally transition from one degree of glory to the next level or next degree of glory, little by little.

We will experience many shifts (large and small), "aha moments" and breakthroughs over time, but the actually working out of our own soul salvation, the process of walking out that breakthrough in our lives day in and day out is always and inevitably a real process.

Truthfully speaking, if we were to receive the fullness of what God has for us prematurely without adequate internal processing and preparation in order to receive it, we will self-sabotage it. "It" within the context of this conversation could be the business, the ministry, the spouse, the vision, the dream and so forth.

Without the soul work and going through little by little, when "it" shows up, no matter how much we prayed and fantasized about it, if we don't feel worthy enough and capable of it or if we have a lot of emotional wounding, we will either run from it or ruin it.

Any blessing or vision that God gives will always involve having healthy relationships with others and will always require a bigger and more mature version of yourself than your current state.

Therefore, we must be expanded or big enough on the inside in order to: 1) receive it and 2) maintain it.

From time to time, God will do a quick work of deliverance and breakthrough, but again more often than not, God works with us just as He did with the ancient Israelites – he incrementally increases us little by little. Once they were out of Egypt they had to conquer many hostile nations and take over their territories. The Israelites were not truly ready to take over and maintain large portions of land. They were not ready to "occupy" the territories fully. Therefore, God had to take them through a gradual incremental process.

We read in Exodus 23:29-30, "I will not drive them out from before you in one year, lest the land become desolate and the beasts of the field become too numerous for you. Little by little I will drive them out from before you, until you have increased, and you inherit the land" (NKJV).

Note, the last phrase – "until you have increased and you inherit the land". They didn't have the capacity to take care of so much land. They didn't have the headcount required to truly possess the land in a way that it could be profitable and maintained.

As it was with the Israelites, so it is with us. God in his graciousness will never give us more than we can bear. We often interpret that phrase in terms of God not placing burdens on us that are more than we can bear, but it actually goes both ways. He will not bless us more than we can bear either or it could crush us.

Another analogy I heard regarding this same principle is that of the tiny closet and the mansion. I've heard it said that we want God to give us a mansion size blessing but, on the inside, we are the size of a 100 square foot closet. In other words, we can't handle a mansion size blessing because our mindsets, emotions and spirits are too small.

Thus, instead of coming up higher in big leaps and bounds, we instead must submit to the process (sometimes not so pretty and often painful) of coming up into new dimensions little by little from one degree of glory to another. This is important because as you maintain and sustain in one dimension, you are then ready for the next dimension.

Sustainability and consistency at one degree of glory is required before we qualify to the next degree. Just like in grade school, unless you are thoroughly tested and examined, you are not allowed to jump two or three grades. You move from kindergarten, to first, second and third grades in sequential order. As you master the concepts at each level, you are promoted.

Just as it is in the natural educational system, so it is with our lives, things of the spirit and personal growth. Remember, it is God who makes the final determination of promotion to the next level according to Psalm 75: 6-7.

Think of it this way, if you stick with the process that God has you on, when you come to this day this time next year your life will be dramatically different. As we heal and order our lives moving from glory to glory, another layer of healing occurs, a new level of wisdom is revealed, new relationships begin to manifest and new things start to happen in our lives.

All of the newness of a new level of glory is in response to the newness and changes within you. Every time, you shed or demolish an old negative belief system (such as a belief in lack and struggle, the belief that you would never find love again, or the belief that you are unworthy and other negative beliefs) a literal spiritual veil is lifted and your clarity of vision and sight is increased.

Let's look back at the scripture right 2 Cor 3: 16 – 18 (AMP):

"Whenever a person turns [in repentance and faith] to the Lord, the veil is taken away. Now the Lord is the Spirit, and where the Spirit of the Lord is, there is liberty [emancipation from bondage, true freedom]. And we all, with unveiled face, continually seeing as in a mirror the glory of the Lord, are progressively being transformed into His image from [one degree of] glory to [even more] glory, which comes from the Lord, [who is] the Spirit."

Every time we change our minds, every time we demolish an old mental or emotional stronghold, because now we know better, a veil is lifted and we move up another degree of glory. This is the crux of coming home. Every layer of healing brings a new level of elevation. When you learn the lesson, you elevate.

Lessons learned equate to wisdom won. Wisdom won equates to purpose. Wisdom gleaned through the process of expanding and elevating the heart through healing, deliverance and purging from the past is a special wisdom that God intends to use for His greater purpose.

Our purpose is to rule, reign and dominate the earth realm. When we begin to fully walk into our rulership and begin to dominate in our personal world, it is imperative that we have the understanding that territories are occupied little by little but once we occupy we must maintain. The territory of your mind, the territory of your will and the territory of your emotions must be brought under subjection to the Spirit of the Living God as the old way, the old rule and system of the flesh is now put under subjugation little by little.

Premature outward elevation in title or external status without inner elevation always results in delay, distraction and destruction. Premature outward elevation before inner territory development will always result in diminished capacity to reign and conquer in life.

Purpose in your heart that this time when you come up higher that your soul will have undergone greater healing and you will have come up higher on the inside first instead of the outside in title or status only to lose it because you didn't have the inner capacity, emotional fortitude and strength to handle it.

REFLECTIVE QUESTIONS

1. When you look back over your life, identify the areas where you have made significant shifts and progress. What new belief, habit or thought process that took root inside of you for this to happen? What thought or belief did you have to give up in order to walk in this new level?
2. Identify the areas where you are still struggling. Ask God to reveal to you the negative belief, the lie or the mental/emotional stronghold or thought pattern that needs to be revealed and released.
3. Your purpose is the area or territory where God has created you to rule and make difference in this world for His Kingdom. It is is revealed in greater clarity every time you up-level in your thought process. In what ways have you seen your purpose begin to become clearer as you started to walk in healing from one degree to the next degree?

PRAYER ACTIVATION

"Heavenly Father, as I begin this journey of ascending into new levels and dimensions help me to remain rooted, grounded, fixed and founded in your love alone. Empower me to stay the course and not get discouraged when changes are not happening as fast as I think they should. Give me wisdom to wait and not prematurely jump ahead of you, but to wait and work with you in the process of elevating to the next dimension. Let me not try to skip steps but allow you to develop me so that I can walk worthy of my calling in a steady and consistent way from glory to glory, strength to strength and faith to faith. In Jesus' name, Amen."

Chapter 14

THE FIVE DEADLY "I'S" THAT PREVENT TRUE CONNECTION

Two are better than one; because they have a good reward for their labour. For if they fall, the one will lift up his fellow: but woe to him that is alone when he falleth; for he hath not another to help him up.

- Eccl. 4: 9-10 (KJV)

*W*omen need healthy connections and relationships.

From my own experience, I believe that there are five deadly "I's" that keep sisters from the connection, collaboration and community necessary for healing and healthy relationships.

They are:

1) Broken Identity
2) Deep Insecurity
3) Feelings of Inadequacy
4) Vain Imaginations
5) Being Easily Intimidated

How do I know these things? Because I have been through every one of them in some form or fashion and I still must carefully guard my heart, ask God to create in me a clean heart and to search my motives. As women of God moving up into new realms and levels, we can't afford to walk around in lack of self-awareness about how we are showing up and what is going on in our hearts when it comes to how we connect with others.

Everything rises and falls on how well we communicate, open up and get along with others for our own personal growth, support and development but also for the Kingdom of God and his purposes.

There is a big difference between being transparent (authentic) and vulnerability. This was a huge shift for me, one that I am still processing. But basically, I can get on a platform, teach, speak, write and so forth about by own issues and struggles (being transparent), but I have more trouble being vulnerable.

I can be transparent and let you look into my life through the window of my transparency and authenticity, so to speak, but I don't have to open the door and actually let you all the way in my life in a much closer way.

Due to the nature of my calling and what God has me talking about – emotional healing, relationships and self-worth, a lot of what I do has to pass through me first before I can share with others.

For me this means that I am not blabbing off telling my acquaintances, family, friends and everyone on Facebook the latest struggle, my latest big victory or anything else I am going through and the revelations or lessons I've learned.

I go through and fall out with God. I process and perhaps tell one or two people. Eventually, my new-found learnings and revelations go into a blog post, teaching or book.

The second thing I've noticed is that I have used being busy as a way of avoiding vulnerability or deeper connection with people (admit, you have too!) I have been severely disappointed in the past by fellow sisters and I am certain I have disappointed them too. So, I would sincerely love and care for them from afar but stay a bit detached in some ways.

I also realized that because my emotions and compassion for people run very deep and strong, I have to be careful who I connect with. I learned that I do not have the personal bandwidth to maintain numerous deep relationships because I care quickly and deeply – even if I don't talk to someone for a while, even if they hurt me, even if they disappoint me, I simply cannot "not" care. Because of this, I keep the number of relationships small.

Not only that, I found that I didn't have the physical and mental capacity to maintain talking to multiple people every day for thirty minutes to an hour, texting back and forth all day and somehow expect to get anything done.

Then I would feel guilty for not properly maintaining close connections. On top of that as I have begun to move further into my calling, I found the way to be a bit lonely at times. As I would attempt to make connections, I found that people would start off okay and then start acting funny.

Inevitably, when I sense that someone is backing off, acting funny, avoiding me or otherwise "appearing" to not be really interested in maintaining a genuine connection with me, this would start the roller coaster ride of the Five Deadly "I's" – Broken Identity, Deep Insecurity, Feelings of Inadequacy, Vain Imaginations and finally being Easily Intimated. Let's break it down.

BROKEN IDENTITY

The crux of the gospel is to redeem, reclaim and restore our broken identity. When we fail to truly embrace our place as Sons and Daughters of God and accept the fact that we are whole, accepted and outrageously loved by God but instead try to prove and perform our way into love, relationships and purpose, we will have broken identities.

Without knowing that:

1) we are accepted in God's love according to (Eph. 1:6)
2) we are chosen and appointed (John 15:16)
3) we are new creatures in Christ (2 Cor. 5:17)

We will inevitably fall into the trap of our identity being rooted in our performance and worldly standards, thus opening ourselves to all of the insecurity and pain that it brings.

Identity is defined as the distinguishing character or personality of an individual; The set of characteristics by which a person or thing is definitively recognizable or known; the state of having unique identifying characteristics held by no other person or thing. (Merriam Webster Online and The Free Dictionary 2/14/18)

Your identity is what makes you. However, if your identity has not been fully developed or broken because you haven't taken the time to go through a healing process to discover who you are and what makes you tick, then you will draw and attract into your life people, places, things and circumstances that are negative.

For the most part, people have a baseline of self-esteem that unless they are very intentional and proactive to continuously heal and grow, they will remain at a certain level.

Without taking the time to heal and become clear of who you are in God and where you are going, it becomes very easy to morph and change your identity to suit other people, please them or be liked by them instead of just simply being yourself.

This typically manifests itself as one part of the five deadly "I's" that keep us from genuine connection primarily as it relates to our self-esteem. If your identity has been wounded or broken in the past by something traumatic, no matter how well put together, articulate, and gifted you are, you can still struggle with esteem issues. I'll be the first to put up my hand and say yes, I have dealt with this!

7 ways this hinders genuine connection is:

1) Exaggerated concern over what people may think
2) Inability to receive compliments
3) Worrying about whether you have treated others badly
4) Anxiety and emotional turmoil; or bouts of depression
5) Emphasis on the negative
6) Sensitivity to criticism
7) Putting on a false front to impress

All of these issues tend to push others away and make it difficult to have authentic connection. Real connection requires being real and being open to receive from others while at the same time being strong enough in who you are that you can stand up, show up and roll with the punches.

It requires having a strong and healthy sense of being loved by God. Most importantly of all, when you make a mistake or receive constructive criticism, or have conflict to be able to not take it so deeply or so personal that your self-esteem plummets or that you cut people off due to having such "thin skin" as a result the low self-esteem.

It is a very vicious cycle that can keep you in bondage not really being able to receive help or criticism because your self-esteem and sense of personal worth is rising and falling based on your mistakes and imperfections that someone may point out or notice.

Real connection, especially those that will challenge you to become better _will require thick skin_. Having a strong personal sense of worthiness and identity means that you can be around someone who is "further along" or knows certain areas better than you do but you can still be with them and feel good about yourself without internalizing every thing and taking things in such a way that it chips at your self-esteem identity.

We often claim that we want to go to the next level, but we don't have the emotional fortitude for it because at the higher levels, the relationships will require more of you to show up as the best version of yourself with higher levels of self-esteem and confidence. At the higher realms and levels, there is no time for being "in your feelings" or "feeling some kind of way" or being easily offended when constructively criticized for your own benefit.

Let me place this one caveat here. Self-esteem and worthiness can ebb and flow depending on what a person is currently going through. In other words, an individual with high self-esteem can go through a hard or difficult season and their self-esteem can diminish as a result of the pain that they went through. Often this is temporary and they will rise again.

In times like this, we have a tendency to take even more things personal, get "in our feelings" and push people away. Again, the season may only last a short time, but the effects of "acting funny" and pushing people away when you are going through a rough time can be very detrimental to God's purpose and destiny for your life.

People can sense that things are wrong, but may not have the understanding, the wisdom or time/capacity to chase you down, make on over you or help you to feel better. This is where we must mature, rise up and take ownership of our feelings and identities, especially during the broken seasons so that we don't inadvertently create further damage in our relationships.

If the identity is broken along with the low self-esteem, a woman of God will have a difficult time maintaining and sustaining true relationships that will push her further into purpose and destiny. Broken identity leads to deep-rooted insecurity.

DEEP INSECURITY & INADEQUACY

If my identity is broken, and I am struggling with low self-esteem, easily offended and feeling less than so I am unable to have real connection, then the natural progression or outcome of that is to become very insecure. Insecurity leads to feelings of inadequacy which is a deep sense of not being good enough.

Let's look at the official definitions of these two words which are incredibly revealing about the nature of these twin deadly "I's".

Insecurity is defined as the state of uncertainty or anxiety about oneself; lack of confidence; self-doubt; the state of being open to danger or threat; lack of protection; to be unstable, rickety, unsteady, or precarious. (Google Dictionary, 2/16/18)

Inadequacy is the state or quality of being inadequate; lack of the quantity or quality required; insufficiency; deficiency; deficit; scarcity; want; lack.

If my whole world view is filtered through the lenses of self-doubt and being unstable within myself along with a profound sense of insufficiency and lack in some area from within, I am a key target for the enemy to work through. Remember, the enemy of our souls work through weak and wounded people. Living in a state of insecurity and inadequacy makes us weak.

When a woman who is insecure and feels inadequate about herself in any way, gets around a confident and happy woman who is flowing in her purpose, the insecure woman will struggle with feelings of jealousy, feel "some kind of way" (not really know why), and sabotage the relationship. Insecurity and Inadequacy are deadly when it comes to having purposeful connections.

Nowhere in the Word of God do we find that this state of being is natural for a believer. Throughout the scriptures we are taught that we are to be rooted in God's love (Eph. 3:17), that we are complete in Him (Col. 2:10), that we are accepted in the beloved (Eph. 1:6) that our adequacy and sufficiency comes from God. (2 Cor. 3:5).

Functioning in a mental and emotional state of insecurity defies the very God we serve and it creates soul level instability on multiple levels. How can we show up in our calling and purposes fully if we are stuck in deep insecurity? How can we operate in relationships in a healthy way without self-sabotaging them due to deep insecurity?

When a woman is deeply insecure about herself or feels a profound sense of inadequacy from within, it tends to manifest itself in four major ways:

1) Being defensive
2) Being controlling
3) Jealousy
4) Having the need for constant validation & reinforcement

All of this is rooted in fear – the fear of not being good enough and that if people see your issues/mistakes they will reject you. The fear is very real and profound especially when there has been significant wounding and rejection in the past. Let's be clear. Most of us at some point have been in this state. It is not an ideal emotional and mental space to stay in for any length of time and the quicker we can get real, be healed and move on from the insecurity and inadequacy the higher level and more quality relationships we can have. Let's look at another area in which our minds work against us when it comes to having healthy relationships.

VAIN IMAGINATIONS

Vain imaginations start off as "they think I'm this or that, they don't like me, they did/said this because of this/that, she did/said/posted that because of this, he probably thinks such and such because of what happened here, she stopped texting because of that, she doesn't call me because of this...she didn't like/heart/share my post because of..." and so forth.

Vain is defined as producing no result; useless. Imagination is the faculty of forming new ideas, or images, or concepts; the part of the mind that imagines things.

Putting the two together you have images, ideas and concepts formed from the natural mind that are useless and produce no results. I would go as far as to say that they do produce results, just not the kind of results you want to see in your life.

Vain imaginations consist of mind movies, assumptions, downright lies, and wild fantasies that we make up in our minds. We can never truly know or understand other people's reason or motives behind what they do. In a way it is prideful to assume that you know why people take certain actions that appear on the surface to be negative or that maybe they may not "like" you. It also speaks to a certain level of immaturity and being overly focused on yourself and personal feelings.

The reality is as previously stated, we cannot tell or know what persons motives are unless we truly operate in the spirit of wisdom and authentic discernment or revelation.

Secondly, most people, nine times out of ten are very preoccupied with their own lives and have not truly paid you any significant attention (sorry, I know it sounds cold, but it's true). The fact that we engage in such endless mind chatter and negativity speaks to the fact that we still have growing up to do if we take things so personal.

The second reality is that we choose the meanings we assign to different situations.

We get to choose how we receive what we see, our reaction, the story we tell ourselves in our head and the meaning that we assign to the situation. In other words, if a person suddenly pulls away, or seems to be less interested in engaging with me on a friendship level, then *I have the power to choose* whether or not I want to spend days re-hashing everything in my mind, getting upset and psychoanalyzing everything trying to figure it out. I get to choose if I am going to "feel some kind of way" every time I see their post on social media or not.

I get to choose the story, the meaning and my response.

The trick is to choose the story, the meaning and the relevant response that is most uplifting, empowering and positive both to myself and to the individual in question.

Until we can master taking ownership and controlling the story in our heads and the meaning, we will be forever at the whim of the vain imaginations that overtake our minds.

In their magazine, The Bottom Line Christian Writers state, "Vain imaginations start with a thought, and if you do not take that thought captive immediately, that thought forms a mental picture in your mind. You then begin "seeing" your fears, anxieties and worries play over and over in your mind. Vain imaginations elicit terror, depression, discouragement, stress, anxiousness, worry and doubt–all of which originate from the enemy. If you choose to hold on to the image the enemy presents to you, it will create a lack of peace and emotional instability."

We are called as believers to do the following when it comes to our thought life:

1) Cast down every thought that exalts itself against the knowledge of God (2 Cor. 10:5)
2) Think on things that are excellent and praiseworthy
3) Keep our minds on God
4) Have the mind of Christ

So often, we do the opposite. Instead we uphold and create strongholds of negative thoughts about other sisters based on how we feel about their behavior or lack thereof; we think on things that are destructive and diminishing to ourselves and others. If we keep our minds on our problems and what we think "they" think of us; and we definitely do not have the mind of Christ.

This is the end result of vain imaginations that spring forth from being deeply insecure and feeling inadequate. This deadly "I" has fractured more authentic connections than you could ever imagine. Last look at the last deadly "I" – being easily intimidated.

EASILY INTIMIDATED

Intimidated is defined as frighten or overawe (someone), especially in order to make them do what one wants. The root meaning of intimidation is to *make timid*.

Timid is defined as showing lack of courage or confidence; easily frightened; apprehensive; afraid; faint-hearted; nervous; or scared.

When we add the specter of being intimidated to the already deadly mix of broken identity, deep insecurity, inadequacy and being overcome by vain imaginations, we have a self-fulfilling, self-imposed state of bondage in place.

When a person is easily intimidated, they are again more prone to people pleasing and doing things out of fear of man than in obedience to God. When a person is easily intimidated, they will not step out in faith to do anything of significance for the Kingdom of God due to fear. When someone is easily intimidated by the progress, momentum and obvious anointing on someone else's life, they can become easily overawed, jealous and offended by that person.

The most insidious aspect of being easily intimidated is the subtle comparison and competition that it breeds. Instead of collaboration and connection, there is comparison and competition between gifts, anointings, ministries, and businesses. When combined with all of the other deadly "I"'s this issue of being intimidated by others is another key way in which Queen's fail to have authentic connections and healthy friendships.

This my sisters, ought not to be.

REFLECTIVE QUESTIONS

1. Out of the five deadly "Is", which one has consistently proven to be an area of struggle or challenge for you? What lesson has God been working in your situation to teach you?
2. Reflect on your strained relationships and begin to sincerely pray for the individuals that we have pushed away as a result of in our insecurities, inadequacies, vain imaginations or being intimidated.
3. In your reflections, think about the times where you got caught up in comparison and competition. What was the end result and what lesson did your soul learn in these situations?

"Heavenly Father, I desire to walk into the fullness of who you have called me to be. I know that this requires that I lay aside every weight that easily besets me (Heb. 12:1-2) and to not operate in the fear of rejection which is the root of these deadly "I's. Show me where I may still be holding grudges and where I am still struggling with a root of rejection that is keeping me from the real connection I genuinely desire and require for this new dimension that you are calling me to. In Jesus' name, Amen."

YOU ARE WORTHY!

Self-worth is the foundation for every great endeavor and is the birthing ground of self-mastery and personal freedom.

– Shannon Tanner

Everything that happens to you is a reflection of what you believe about yourself. We cannot outperform our level of self-esteem. We cannot draw to ourselves more than we think we are worth.

– Iyanla Vanzant

The two quotes above succinctly sum up everything.

The only way to effectively ascend to the next dimension of your journey as a woman is to ascend from a deep place of knowing you are worthy.

Your personal sense of self-worth as a child of God, a daughter of the King is the foundation and the starting point for every God idea, vision and dream. For if you do not believe you are worthy of being more, doing more, and having more, you will not be able to effectively walk out these 14 keys of ascending.

Self-mastery, i.e., the ability to walk in self-control which is also a fruit of the spirit, is required to navigate the atmosphere and the challenges of the next dimension.

Experiencing true personal freedom – the freedom Christ provided by His completed work on the cross is without question a mandatory requirement for those who wish to come up higher. Personal freedom is the liberty to be and do all that God has called you to be without the fear of man.

Lastly, we truly cannot outperform or outdo beyond what we deeply believe about ourselves. Our lives provide a mirror to what we *really* believe at a subconscious level, more than what we are saying out of our mouths. Remember, life doesn't happen *to us*, it flows through *us*. We simply cannot outrun our own belief systems.

The biggest demons we fight against is not fornication, alcoholism, drugs, stealing, etc. I would go as far as to say that it is not fear. The two biggest demons we face is unworthiness and shame.

If we didn't struggle with the shame, the hiding out, and the embarrassment from thinking we are not good enough or unworthy because of unconscious beliefs (lies), emotional wounds, and traumas, the outer behavior would line up.

If we deeply knew our worth and value, then we would believe and act accordingly. Eventually we would manifest our true purpose.

I encourage you on today as I do myself, to keep digging deep. Continue to work out your own soul salvation so that you can walk worthy of the calling. Every tear, every struggle, every investment that you make into healing your life and walking in purpose is worth it. Know that you are not alone in this journey to the next level. Where you are now is not your final destination. This is not your home. As you ascend higher and higher into your purpose, you are ascending to your true *home*. Enjoy the journey. You are worthy!

ENDNOTES

Chapter 1
Bishop R. C. Blakes, Jr. Queenlogy. Untapped Potential Publishing June 14, 2017.

Chapter 3
Bishop R. C. Blakes, Jr. Queenlogy. Untapped Potential Publishing June 14, 2017.
Dr. Cindy Trimm. The Prosperous Soul: Your Journey to a Richer Life. Destiny Image. March 17, 2015.

Chapter 4
Joyce Meyer. The Everyday Life Bible. Faithwords. April 10, 2018.
Dr. Cindy Trimm. The Prosperous Soul: Your Journey to a Richer Life. Destiny Image. March 17, 2015

Chapter 6
Christine Arylo. Choosing Me Before We. New World Library. February 1, 2009

Chapter 8
Dr. Cindy Trimm. The Prosperous Soul: Your Journey to a Richer Life. Destiny Image. March 17, 2015

Chapter 10
Craig Groeschel. Divine Direction: 7 Decisions That Will Change Your Life. February 7, 2017.
Osazee Thompson. Precision Purpose: Enjoying the Signature Life You Were Born To Live. December 10, 2013.

Chapter 14
Top Ten Facts About Low Self Esteem. Mark Tyrell. Article. www.self-confidenc.co.uk.

Overcoming Vain Imaginations. The Bottom Line Christian Writers. www.tblfaithnews.com

You Are Worthy
Shannon Tanner. Worthy: The Power of Wholeness. Three Eight Media Group. April 24, 2014.

Quotes from the sources above were retrieved or accessed between 1/1/18 – 2/19/18.

Quotes from various individuals at the top of each chapter and throughout were retrieved either from personal memory or Google searches during the period above as well.

Words defined herein were accessed from either The Free Dictionary at www.thefreedictionary.com or Dictionary by Merriam-Webster at www.merriam-webster.com from 1/1/18 – 02/19/18

ACKNOWLEDGEMENTS

I thank God for my life, my salvation and the opportunity to live, love and serve. I am eternally grateful and thankful to Him.

I'd also like to acknowledge my parents, the late great Rev. Gerald L. Tillman and my mother, Linda Tillman. Without the firm foundation of faith and love instilled in me from such a young age, I do not know where I would be.

I am grateful for my loving and brilliant sister, Myra Thomas who has always been incredibly loving and supportive of me as well as my best friend of over 25 years, Cassandra Hall – a caring and loving soul.

I am thankful for my two sons, Michael & Trey - now grown young men who have seen me at my absolute worse and they still love me.

A special thank you to Carla Cannon and the team at Cannon Publishing for bringing my second book project to life! We have come full circle!

Time and space does not permit for me to properly acknowledge all of my family, friends, supporters, followers and colleagues in my journey, however I do want to thank a special mentor, Shannon Evette in whom I first deeply learned the true meaning of personal wholeness and worthiness. I never heard of this concept at the level and depth in which Shannon taught and my life has never been the same.

I love all of you.

Tonika Maria

ABOUT THE AUTHOR

Tonika Breeden is a Certified Christian Life Coach and Certified HISCoach, author, speaker and mentor who loves to use her passion for practical wisdom and truth to help Christian women successfully navigate tough relationship transitions and "wilderness seasons" with peace, clarity and greater levels of wholeness.

From her own wilderness season of seeking to be married without being whole in Christ first, she learned the hard way on how to walk in wholeness and completeness in Christ. Because of that, her desire is to help women become rooted, grounded, fixed and founded in the love of God before seeking to be married.

Her gift of writing has been well-developed for many years, however, it was the unexpected and untimely death of her father which served as a wake-up call for her to get real, be healed and move on from a dead-end relationship so that she could fully walk in her purpose and destiny and no longer waste time.

In addition to her passion and focus on healthy romantic relationships, her deepest passion is to see women walk in emotional wholeness through the process of simply getting real and being healed. Through her teaching and writing, Tonika has helped hundreds of women get real, be healed and move on in their lives so that they could walk in emotional healing, resiliency and mastery.

Tonika has led and spoken into the lives of many women through numerous small groups, church conferences, workshops and both live and virtual events. She has been privileged to speak via closed livestream to a growing group of followers in Lusaka, Zambia and other African countries who deeply need the message of healthy relationships and emotional healing.

With a strong general business and accounting background, Tonika is a senior accountant for a software company in the greater Raleigh area. She is an avid reader, blogger, and bible study curriculum writer and prayer team member in her church. She resides in Durham, NC with her two sons.

Stay Connected with Tonika!

Website www.tonikabreeden.com
Facebook www.facebook.com/getrealbehealed)
Twitter and Instagram @GetRealBeHealed

If you desire private coaching services, would like for Tonika to speak at your event or would like to participate in any of Tonika's live group coaching communities, email her at info@tonikabreeden.com

Receive FREE audio teachings on the 14 Keys to Ascending to the Next Dimension by subscribing at bit.ly/awomansjourney
Also Available on Amazon in Kindle & Paperback

Get Out of that Dead-End Relationship NOW! *A Christian Woman's Guide on How to Get Real, Healed and Move On*